EVERYDAY CUBA FOR NON-CUBANS: BEYOND THE RESORT CLICHÉ

A Perspective on Contemporary Cuban Society, Struggles, and Opportunities for Economic Growth

Araz Jahani

Published By: Trulysis Publishing Inc.
6428 Yonge Street, PO Box 69565
Toronto, ON, Canada, M2M-4K3
www.Trulysis.com
www.EverydayCubaforNonCubans.com/

ISBN: 978-1-7773052-4-6 (Hardcover)
ISBN: 978-1-7773052-1-5 (Paperback)

Book Cover and Map Design: Snir Alayof

DEDICATION

This book is dedicated to my family, especially to my Father, Mother and Brother, for their continued support, for encouraging me to think outside the box and stick to my beliefs.

Además, este libro está dedicado a la isla mágica y al pueblo valiente, hermano y orgulloso de Cuba, que me ha aceptado con el corazón puro y los brazos abiertos. También se lo dedico a los guajiros dichosos que luchan todos los días con su sudor para mejorar su país. Una dedicación especial a la orgullosa holguinera que me abrió los ojos, me enseñó todo sobre la historia cubana y me mostró todo sobre esta isla mágica.

Hasta la verdad siempre…

CONTENTS

"La verdad, una vez despierta, no vuelve a dormirse".

"The truth, once awakened, does not fall back asleep."

José Martí

PREFACE

My first trip to Cuba took place in 2004. Since then, I've returned multiple times and have met countless travelers that make infinite assumptions about what the real Cuban life is like outside the resorts.

Travelers make assumptions about the realities of Cuba either based on their brief chats with resort employees, conversations with tour guides, or their occasional interactions with the locals outside the touristic areas. Interactions with the locals are only possible in Havana and Varadero, and this is usually as close as tourists get to the truth, as these two locations are in the mainland part of Cuba. Other locations, such as resorts in Guardalavaca, are approximately a 60 km taxi ride to the closest city of Holguín. Similarly, Cayo Coco is around 60 km to the city of Morón. To make matters worse, Cayo Santa María is over 100 km from the city of Santa Clara. As a result, the tourists don't see the real Cuba much and, if they do, they don't have the opportunity to experience and absorb it.

This is what motivated me to write this book. I wanted to provide anyone interested in Cuba, including travelers, with real information about the current reality experienced by the Cuban people, not only in a descriptive fashion, but rather by addressing the root causes of said reality. In order to provide a proper understanding of contemporary Cuba, I decided to not simply throw the reader into the fire but instead offer an introduction to the history of Cuba that provides some perspectives around the state of affairs and people's lives.

Beyond simply analyzing the root causes of the economic situation in Cuba, I also discuss potential opportunities for economic growth based on my knowledge, research, and personal experiences travelling through the country and meeting its people.

This book intends to inform the reader regarding the reality experienced by Cuban citizens every day, equipping them with the tools and knowledge to draw informed conclusions. The intent is to give the readers 20% knowledge so that they can make 80% of their assumptions more accurately. More importantly, this book is intended to prepare every traveler or anyone interested in learning more about Cuba to understand the realities of the country and set the correct expectations of the economic shortcomings that are masked by the walls of the resorts.

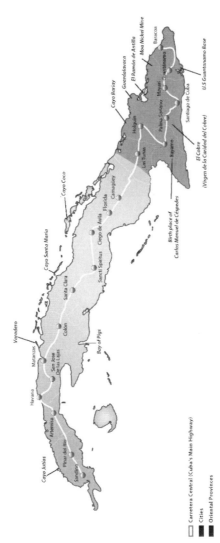

Figure 1. Map of Cuba.

CHAPTER I: MY FIRST TIME ON THE MAGICAL ISLAND

It was a dreary, rainy, summer morning in Toronto, Canada. Mother Nature was not feeling gregarious, given the severe thunderstorms and flash floods. My friends and I were running late to catch the 6 am flight from Toronto Pearson International Airport. Our summer was a write-off, and it was a great time to get away from the inclement weather, since we couldn't swim in the lakes, go on camping trips, or participate in other fun idiosyncratically Canadian activities that we would typically engage in. Outside of the United States and Canada, this was to be my first real vacation abroad. Considering I had just had the convocation of an immensely rigorous and, at times, intractable four-year engineering program, this trip was long overdue. The car was getting closer to the airport. Although the persistent rain made me happy to be getting away, I did not know what to expect upon arrival at my destination.

A few hours into the flight, I looked out the plane window and noticed that we were over the Florida Keys. The sun rays were reflecting through the tiny waves of a calm ocean, and the air looked like a crystal glass with no impurities. The view manifested a sense of calmness, of profound relaxation, a sensation that nothing mattered in life except this infinite beauty. The view instilled liberty from all of the problems that occupied my mind. I felt euphoria as the sun rays penetrated the window into the plane. There were no more gloomy clouds, rain, or thunderstorms. This calmness made me fall asleep.

Upon landing, I woke up, and all I saw were two signs that read "Bienvenido al Aeropuerto Internacional Juan G. Gómez – Varadero",[1] and a poster that read "Socialismo o Muerte."[2] I was in Cuba.

My friends and I were staying at a newly built resort on the scenic Varadero beach strip. At the time, we could only stay at hotels. Once I arrived at the hotel, I met up with my brother and his friends, and after checking in immediately rushed to the beach. Expecting dark sand and cold water, as I was accustomed to in Canada, I asked my brother how cold the water was. In a deadpan tone, he responded, "The water is freezing like in Wasaga Beach."[3] However, I realized immediately after inserting my feet in the water that his reply was far from the truth.

It was beyond belief. I was experiencing a natural hot tub, but at the shores of a vast, turquoise ocean. With white sand and palm trees in my line of sight, I watched jovial vacationers and locals enjoyed themselves under the cloudless sky. On top of that, an array of colorful fish was darting around my feet. I thought I was in paradise.

While I was taking in my new surroundings, my curiosity kicked in, and I began to wonder why everyone appeared so exuberant and why everything seemed so utopian. After spending a couple of days at the hotel, my friends and I decided to explore the town of Varadero, both to look around the key sights, and to speak with the local Cubans and get an idea of their sentiment towards their homeland.

---

[1] Welcome to the Juan G. Gómez International Airport – Varadero.

[2] Socialism or Death.

3 Wasaga beach is a tourist beach town in Ontario, Canada.

While we walked around Varadero, we met Cubans who were mostly working in restaurants and bars. Most of the people who worked in Varadero were usually from the nearby non-tourist towns of Cárdenas, Santa Marta or Matanzas. I was excited to hear stories about how life really was outside of the resort.

I met Juan, a young mechanical engineering student from the University of Matanzas who was working as a bartender at a nearby restaurant. He had completed the second year of his engineering program, and during his summer break he decided to take on a new job to make some extra cash. He was a very humble, good-hearted and yet shy person, and I believe part of his timidness was due to the fact that he recently started learning English and was not confident about his new language skills. He told me that he loved studying mechanical engineering and that, as part of his schoolwork, he had done exciting projects with real-world applications. However, he told me that he was considering not continuing his program but instead switching to tourism so he could work in hotels. His reasons were that he did not foresee a career in mechanical engineering that would allow him to work in the specific field that he was interested in. His hesitation to continue his studies resulted from the fact that no state-run companies that were specialized in the aerospace sector existed. Juan said that he didn't believe a career in mechanical engineering would make him enough money to support his family, and switching to tourism would enable him to work at the hotels and make money from tips.

As I wrapped up my conversation with Juan and left the restaurant, my friends and I started to walk down Varadero's main street (Avenida 1ra). As we were walking, we were approached by two young men who started the conversation with: "Hello my friend," and then immediately after: "Where are you from?". These two young men were from the town of Cárdenas and they wanted to sell us Cuban cigars. They were trying to assure one of my friends who was a smoker that what they were trying to sell was not rolled-up banana leaves, but authentic Cuban cigars. Even though our group of friends included only one smoker, he did not end up buying anything from the young men. Instead, we invited them to have a drink with us and chat more. They eventually opened up and told us that one of the young men's mother worked at the cigar factory and she was taking the boxes of cigars with the official guarantee seals. These two guys were then bringing the merchandise to Varadero to sell to the tourists on the streets, but they had to be cautious so as to not draw attention from the authorities. They mentioned that the money from selling the cigars was helping them put food on the table and save up, little by little, to buy an electric water heater for their shower. They told me that in Cuba the majority of the houses do not have hot water and that pretty much everyone takes a shower with cold water. If they wanted to use hot water, they usually had to boil it in a big pot and mix it with cold water, and then pour it over their body.

After our conversations with these two young men, we headed over to the artisan market and I met Miguel, who is one of the most talented individuals I have ever met. He was a true artist who carved wooden statues with incredible attention to detail. Miguel and his son worked together carving wooden statues, and made their money by selling their artistic talent. Miguel mentioned that half of his family, including his two older daughters, lived in South Florida. When I asked him if he wanted to go and live in the United States, he told me that he never wants to leave Cuba but he would love to visit the U.S. one day. He told me that he had established his life in Varadero, and with the income from his art sale plus the occasional remittances sent by his daughters, he had a better and more relaxing life there than the one he might have had if he had chosen to move to the U.S. I admired Miguel's work and I immediately became his customer by purchasing a statue of an Afro Cuban (Mulata) woman which I still hold to this day.

When we got back to our hotel, our friendly lifeguard, who was always smiling, greeted us by the pool. His stories were always interesting. He used to tell us about the difficulties he had providing food for his family, and he sold whatever he could to the tourists to be able to support them. He told us about how he wanted to leave the country on a raft and bring his friends, as each of them added value to the journey. He, as a lifeguard, would be able to swim while his other friends were sailors and could direct the raft to the U.S. However, he mentioned that he had put his plans on hold because some of his friends who had already left for the U.S. did not make it and, according to him, either died of dehydration or were attacked by sharks. At the time of my conversations with our lifeguard in 2004, because of the "Wet feet, dry feet" policy of the U.S., many Cubans risked their lives on the Straits of Florida crossing. The policy was later discontinued in 2017 by President Obama. The discontinuation of this policy, however, did not stop the rafts from going to the U.S., but the numbers have reduced ever since. Three years after I met our happy lifeguard friend, we were told that he met an Italian woman in the resort, got married, and moved to Italy.

At the hotel, I also met a Cuban diplomat who had traveled all over the world. He and his family were staying there at a time (in 2004) when Cubans were not even permitted to enter the hotels. However, I believe he was being rewarded for his contribution and service to the state. I enjoyed listening to his travel stories about his time as a student in the former USSR, and his diplomatic work in various African and European countries. We chatted about diverse topics such as Cuba's medical system, society and economy, even though my knowledge was limited at that time about these subjects. The gentleman was a proud revolutionary who praised Cuba for its positive contribution to Cubans in terms of medicine, as well as free education and healthcare.

My walk around Varadero had resulted in meeting a

diverse group of folks in Cuba from all walks of life, and this provided me with a holistic view of life in this newly discovered paradise. This holistic view was constituted by 20% facts and 80% assumptions that I had made about life outside of the resort.

I also met quite a few tourists who were in love with Cuba, who never hesitated to come back to this paradise. It was clear that I was not alone in thinking this place was paradisiacal. However, I did not feel I had enough insight as to what life here actually was like. I wondered why visitors really fell in love with it. Was it the fish darting beneath their feet and the people-watching? Was it the palm trees and laid-back atmosphere? What made Cuba more attractive than the Dominican Republic or Hawaii or the Bahamas, and why were there more happy faces on the streets of Varadero, Matanzas, and Holguín than on the streets of Toronto, Vancouver, or New York City? These questions, though formulated at the ripe age of 23, have drawn me back to Cuba many times in order to expand my understanding of the underlying social, cultural, economic, and political idiosyncrasies of this country.

I now know that the jovial passersby that I watched from my vista on my first trip were mostly tourists, enjoying the tranquil and aesthetically pleasing beaches under the cloudless skies that seemed ever-present. Some of them probably sought out Cuba as a travel destination because they were intrigued by a country so close to the Americas with such a different economic system, and because they wanted to experience something outside of the normal destinations. Others, I'm sure, wanted to try and meet their significant other or make long-lasting friendships in the name of adventure. In some ways, these people and I were similar. However, the majority of tourists kept to their resorts and cocktails by the beach, confining themselves to the paradise version of Cuba, with shops and restaurants sustaining the paradise vibe. These patrons never saw the day-to-day of the non-paradise, tourist-infested Cuba, so naturally, they missed out on the unique culture, institutional setup, and underlying Cuban lifestyle, whether by choice or not.

I was different from other travelers. A few days into my trip, I had already found myself to be immensely curious. It always felt as if the hotels were acting as a shield, insulating me from what might happen if I stepped outside the bubble. What was on the other side? How could I get an accurate understanding of life in the Cuban cities and countryside which are far less traveled? Without getting out of the resorts, living like a local, and interacting with the local Cubans, I felt as if I could have traveled to any other country in the Caribbean to get the white sand, palm trees, and "paradise" vibes. To visit Cuba, I needed an understanding and perspective which only comes as a byproduct of immersing yourself in interactions with the people outside of the bubble meant to keep the paradise-seekers in. One cannot define the box from within, but by stepping outside, one can begin to obtain an accurate perspective of reality.

Every human on this earth has a unique life story. People are naturally prone to cognitive biases and make assumptions based on how social information has been passed on to them through their network. Humans generalize and don't always seek to zoom in to understand each and every person's thought journey. As such, we take mental shortcuts based on media, conversations, and more. Assumptions are derived from our mental models, which generally help our brains to classify and simplify information. Our mental models are usually accurate most of the time. Still, there are gaps in every mental model, and 20% of these gaps generally result in 80% of our misunderstandings and assumptions that we form about any given situation, or, in this case, about a country and its people. As a result, there is a gap between our assumptions and reality. I reminded myself of these ideas when exploring Cuba and purposely chose not to make assumptions about Cuban society, its institutions, social norms, or the effects of the Cuban revolution and its socio-cultural and socio-economic consequences. I sought to have a more open mind, in order to see for myself first-hand.

I remember asking various tourists what their stereotypes of Cuba were before visiting, because I certainly had my own prior to my first visit. I heard it all. One of them assumed that Cuba had a free healthcare system that was one of the most outstanding in the world. Another said that they thought that the current economic system in Cuba had helped the development of human capital. Some said the opposite. Others said that Cubans had access to free housing. As for myself, I had assumed that the government would guarantee its people access to basic needs, including fresh organic food, clothing, and transportation, based on the political system I knew Cuba operated under. Furthermore, I thought its political structure might have created a different level of thinking which helped to advance cultural activities and reduced stress for Cubans. Knowing that people often generalize, I decided to seek a deeper understanding of Cuban culture, in an attempt to validate or invalidate any of my preconceived notions. I sought to visit *las calles* (the streets) and *el campo* (the countryside), and as a result, I gained invaluable life experiences and a wealth of knowledge.

It is my hope that the anecdotes and analysis that grew from these experiences will help portray the real Cuba. My goal is for readers to understand Cuban culture, the economic challenges it faces, and most importantly, to explore the what and the why of Cuba's present-day form. Only by first looking at the *what* of Cuba can we begin to delve into the *why*. It will begin to make sense why, although Cuba has its fair share of economic and societal issues, there is an unbelievable infatuation with it.

¡Vamos![4]

---

[4] Let's go!

CHAPTER II: LIFESTYLE DIFFERENCES BETWEEN NORTH AMERICA AND CUBA

There is nothing like the euphoria that comes with being in a tropical environment with the blazing sun, white sand, turquoise water, and the calming sound of the ocean breeze. It is the reason why, since my first trip to Cuba, I have expanded my travels to the Dominican Republic, Caribbean side of Mexico, the Florida Keys, and to other parts of the Caribbean. My visits were not only motivated by meditation, yoga, walking, peak state rituals, or even the natural beauty, but also by the upbeat, genuine, and exultant culture which kept drawing me to that part of the world. When I started to work as an Engineer and had more money to travel, I decided to go to the Caribbean at least once per year. My trips usually happened during the New Year's holidays, mainly to Cuba, because it was the most economical option to get some sun and escape the usual 20 cm of snow and frigid temperatures that Toronto played host to. As a result of my frequent visits, I was able to travel to Cuba, staying at various resorts in different parts of the country. I traveled to all of the cities in western Cuba, such as Pinar Del Río, as well as to the easternmost part of Cuba—the provinces of Holguín and Santiago de Cuba. Initially, Varadero was my favorite spot because of the party scene and its proximity to Havana.

Although I had limited vacation days with my employer at the time, the frequency of these travels increased gradually when I started working for BlackBerry during its years of rapid growth. This also meant that my trips were not only for personal reasons, but rather for business, as the usage of the BlackBerry Messenger (BBM) was booming in Latin America, and BlackBerry sales were rising significantly. BlackBerry had established a fully dedicated team to oversee Latin American operations by creating the BlackBerry head offices in South Florida and, as a young Project Manager, I had the privilege to travel to the Fort Lauderdale/Miami area almost every month. The Latin American Manager position was a role that I took up in order to be exposed to a region whose culture and people sparked my curiosity.

As the only non-Latino member of the project office in South Florida, I initially felt out of place because of my inability to speak Spanish. Through a combination of starting Spanish classes, having meetings with Spanish speakers, and taking frequent trips to Latin America, I managed to pick up the language.

The crux of my Spanish language-learning efforts happened in Bogotá, Colombia. I remember being at the famous "Juan Valdez Café" coffee shop the day after arriving in Bogotá and standing in a long line up of people waiting to get their breakfast and morning coffee. The cashier was asking the customers for orders, but with accents and words that were different from what I was taught in my Spanish classes in Canada. It seemed that no one spoke a word of English, which admittedly did make me nervous. I was starving and needed my morning coffee and didn't want to backpedal, despite being nervous about trying my Spanish for one of the first times outside of a formal classroom setting.

When it was my turn, I looked back and saw the long queue behind me, and it felt as if everyone was watching. I was quick to remind myself that I had studied Spanish for a year, which eased the nervousness a bit. I led with, "¿Puedo pedir un espresso con arepita con queso por favor?"[5] The journey had begun.

I was, of course, having to speak to everyone in Spanish, from ordering taxis to doing my laundry to grocery shopping. One of the most memorable stories is of my haggling skills when purchasing a souvenir for my mom. The local shopkeeper, whom I was buying the souvenirs from, was one of many near the famous Monserrate church in Bogotá. At the time, I was confidently haggling, and I felt that I was getting a great deal on my purchases. However, it turned out that I had paid quite a bit more than I should have because I had mixed up how to count. Being in Bogotá allowed me to learn from these experiences and exposed me to the language first-hand in a non-classroom setting. By being forced to speak Spanish, I quickly learned that the best way to learn a language is to jump right in, and in my situation, I quickly lost my fear of speaking it.

Besides work, I was in Bogotá because I wanted to meet up with a former colleague of mine, an intelligent, beautiful, outgoing Colombian girl from Pasto who used to reside in an upscale and aesthetically pleasing area of Bogotá. She accelerated my Spanish skills by throwing me into the deep end, continuously choosing to speak only Spanish to me. I didn't just learn the Spanish language from her though. I learned from the positive aspects of her personality and her outlook on life. She was bubbly, warm, and extroverted and had no fear of sharing details of her personal life with me, despite the fact that we did not know each other very well

---

[5] May I order an espresso with *arepita* (a type of food made of ground maize dough) with cheese, please?

at the time. Her personality and approach towards life was a contrast to what I had observed in the big North American cities like Toronto or New York, where people tend to keep to themselves and do not typically trust others right away. This warm and friendly personality was the start of a pattern I began to notice in most Latin American countries. I remember being in an elevator with a stranger, and upon leaving, they said "Have a great day." After observing my friend's personality and running into situations with strangers like the one in the elevator, I began to wonder, why do these people seem more open in comparison to folks in North America? Is it their outlook on life? Is being happy a choice or does it have more to do with the intrinsic wiring of a person?

Fast forward a few years, after the fall of BlackBerry and loss of its popularity due to the rising competition from Apple iPhone/iOS and Android-based phones, I was laid off from the company that I loved. When this happened, my approach to the corporate world changed. I began to think that one's tenure with a company did not matter, nor did the working relationships that one invested so much time and energy in over the years. The timesheets and the hours invested beyond what was expected to climb the corporate ladder didn't mean as much to me as I had previously thought. I had somewhat of a paradigm shift in my thinking, in that I began to approach life more freely and focused more on happiness and balance.

In the end, what matters most is time with family and friends. Work was often an excuse for missing key life events. Many people, throughout the years in my tenure at Blackberry, lost their significant other and their relationships over lack of work-life balance. After my time at BlackBerry, I felt that I had gained some good work experience but that I had lost a lot in the process. I didn't want to make that mistake again. I remember doing the math on the number of hours I spent at work versus the net benefit to myself and my family, and wondering why I had not had this shift sooner.

Getting laid off was a blessing in disguise, and this unexpected life transformation led me to pursue work as an independent consultant rather than a full-time employee. I had decided to pursue the independent consulting career path for more financial freedom, but also to have the option to be able to travel when I wanted to and spend more time with my family and friends.

In a society like Cuba's, because of its different economic system, a "work to live" lifestyle creates and nurtures a different value system in people. By referring to a "work to live" lifestyle in Cuba, I am not implying that people are economically well off by North American standards. On the contrary, this is not the case in Cuba, given the harsh economic conditions that the Cuban people have endured over the years. Remarkably, considering the difficult living conditions, financial instability, shortage of food and commodities, lack of adequate infrastructure, and many other problems, people carry on with their lives and seem to make the most of it. On average, they have more time to spend with their families and more time to interact with their neighbors. A common assumption made by some tourists is that Cubans seem to be on average more content with what they have than an average person from North America, despite the difficult living conditions of Cubans in comparison to those in North America. It's possible that lower workplace stress, limited politics, and the absence of the North American rat race geared towards climbing the corporate ladder are all factors at play.

One may think that the socialist economic system provides the foundations for a "work to live" lifestyle. Others may argue that in a communist state, there is no incentive for competition. Consequently, there is no economic stimulation and improvement, and accordingly, Cubans do not need to work as hard as North Americans, allowing them to have more time to dedicate to other aspects of life. Others may disagree and hold an opinion that Cuba promotes competition, specifically in the fields of arts, ballet, and sports. To analyze today's Cuba, we need to understand Cuban society, and to understand Cuban society, we first need to explore Cuban history over the years to see how it got to where it is today. I will focus less on the events surrounding the 1959 revolution, as most people are familiar with that. Instead, I'll go all the way back to when Christopher Columbus first discovered America by setting foot on Bahía de Bariay, in the province of Holguín, Cuba.

CHAPTER III: *LA LUCHA POR LA INDEPENDENCIA* - THE STRUGGLE FOR INDEPENDENCE

"No hay hombre sin Patria ni Patria sin Libertad".

"There is no man without a Country, nor a Country without freedom."

José Martí

The best way to understand the present is to study the past. In order to understand how Cuba functions today, we must go back in time to some of the key moments in its history. This includes the arrival of the Spaniards to the New World and their subsequent dominance and control of the sugar and tobacco businesses, not to mention the horrendous enslavement of indigenous populations through which they created an environment of tyranny, inequality, and abuse. This led to centuries of injustices and outside pressures that limited autonomy and prevented Cuba from determining its own future. The population was split into a *Haute Bourgeoisie* who were in control of the wealth and were concentrated in the western part, and the rest of the population who struggled to feed their families. This led to another key moment, the Cuban Independence Movement that culminated with the Spanish-American War of 1898, when U.S. forces intervened, allowing the island to secure its independence from Spain. Finally, one last key moment in Cuban history is the Revolution of 1959, after Batista's dictatorial regime which was characterized by a lack of equality and opportunity, and a widening of the considerable gap in wealth distribution across the country.

The discovery of the American continent, and the discovery of Cuba as one of the first places in the Americas, was a turning point in the history of humanity. The New World offered opportunities that the Old World would benefit from for centuries to come. It also has brought human torment, catastrophe, slavery, and injustice.

It all started when Christopher Columbus landed in Cayo Bariay in the province of Holguín, Cuba. On Sunday, October 28, 1492, when Columbus landed in the Bay of Bariay, he said that Cuba was "the most beautiful land human eyes have ever seen" (Oppmann, 2019). At that time, the native population of Cuba, the Taíno and the Siboney people, were farming the land for tobacco, cassava (yuca), peanuts, and sweet potatoes, while also catching fish. The Spaniards, or *Conquistadores* (the conquerors), brought diseases such as smallpox and measles, which resulted in the deaths of many Taíno people (Baker, 2019). At this time, the Spaniards proceeded to enslave, kill, and work to death many of the Taíno people. As a result, virtually all of the indigenous population was wiped out.

Because tobacco was in high demand and had become one of the main exports of the new world, the conquerors enslaved the indigenous people, forcing them to work in the tobacco fields and reaping the rewards of their free labor. The Spaniards loaded their ships with all of the treasures of Latin America, such as gold, silver, precious stones, and spices, and reunited at the strategic port of Havana before heading back to Spain. Along with these, the Spaniards also loaded the precious tobacco and sugar, produced by the sweat of the Taíno, and set on their journey back to their motherland. Thus, Havana, because of its strategic position, became the central commercial hub of the Caribbean (Schneider, 2018).

Much of the local slave population ended up disappearing because they were either worked to death or killed by diseases. As a result, to keep production and the benefits of free labor, the Spaniards chose to import slaves from Africa. With the importation of slaves from Africa, which eventually outnumbered the Spaniards in Cuba, the conquerors now had the ability to run their lucrative tobacco and sugar businesses (Ted A. Henken, 2013).

The slaves from Africa not only brought their skills to work on the farms, but also their cultural and religious beliefs. These were often seen by the Spaniards as a threat to Catholicism and to the dominant Spanish cultural practices they imposed. Despite the pressures from the Spaniards, African slaves managed to preserve their cultural practices, leading to the birth of a unique Afro-Cuban culture and set of beliefs. The details of the Afro-Cuban culture and its religion, Santería, are further explained in Appendix I.

Why did the Spaniards focus on the sugar business, and how did this business boom in Cuba?

Haiti, at the time a French colony, was the leading exporter of sugar. However, the slaves in Haiti rebelled against their masters and liberated themselves in 1804, closing the sugar plantations (Dubois, March 2004). This event caused the plantation owners in Haiti to go to Cuba to re-establish their business there. The Spaniards, who were ruling Cuba at that time, welcomed this expansion into the sugar business because it brought a new source of revenue. Even though they had systematically robbed the treasures of Latin America, the Spaniards continued their heavy taxes and exploitation of Cuba to advance their lagging economy at home.

The sugar business divided Cuba into virtually two parts: the richer western part of Cuba, with Havana at the center, which enjoyed the profits of the sugar business, and the eastern region, where the production and farming of sugar cane fueled the gains realized by the owners in the western part (Schneider, 2018).

One may think that the same rebellion that occurred in Haiti may have also happened in Cuba because of the horrendous treatment of the slaves. This was the case, but the uprising did not start with the actual slaves. Instead, it started with a sugar business owner who was tired of paying excessive tax, dealing with corruption, and deprivation of religious liberty in Cuba (Foner, 1963). This sugar business owner liberated all of his slaves and told everyone to rebel against the Spaniards. This brave man's name was Carlos Manuel de Céspedes, and this is the Céspedes that ended up declaring Cuba as an independent nation and formed an army with his newly freed slaves to go to war with the Spaniards. The rebels, under the leadership of Carlos Manuel de Céspedes, managed to win over eastern Cuba. The Spaniards feared that the rebels might get close to the western part, so they tried to isolate the west from the east by concentrating the Spanish army at the center of Cuba. Unfortunately, in one of the battles, Carlos Manuel de Céspedes was killed, and his army of rebels could not win the war against the Spaniards. Subsequently, there were reforms made by the Spaniards to ease the tension and improve labor conditions. However, many of the rebels were executed, and some fled the country, mostly to the United States. The Spaniards put the remaining rebels into work camps, and in these camps, life for the rebels was, for lack of a better word, miserable.

The Cuban rebels at that time consisted of various factions led by mainly four men: Máximo Gómez, Antonio Maceo, Calixto García, and a young poet by the name of José Martí. Martí is considered a Cuban hero for unifying all of the rebel leaders and planning to wage war against the

Spaniards to make Cuba independent from Spanish rule. Martí was also a famous poet, not only in Cuba but in the entire Spanish speaking world in the 19th century. He was one of the rebels who was put in the work camps by the Spaniards and later resided in the United States, who, along with Máximo Gómez and Antonio Maceo, planned "The War of Independence" against the Spaniards in 1868 (Mauricio Augusto Font, 2006).

In my opinion, Martí was not only a philosopher, a poet, and a Cuban hero, but he displayed deep and formidable business strategy expertise because of his realization that the war needed money if it was to be successful. Therefore, he and his team decided to reach out to the Cubans exiled in Florida (mainly in the Tampa area and Key West) to raise funds for their war. They used the money to finance the war initially by buying weapons and sending them to Cuba to arm the people on the ground. Once the people were armed, José Martí and his ships began to set sail from the U.S. to eastern Cuba.

Consequently, the war of independence started in the east, near the city of Baracoa in the province of Guantanamo. Interestingly, some of the wealthy landowners had actually volunteered their slaves to participate in the struggle for independence. Prior to the war, Martí and his team had authored the Manifesto of Montecristi, which outlined how the war should be run. One of the primary principals of this Manifesto was that blacks and whites alike should participate in the struggle for independence.

Unfortunately, Martí was martyred in a battle against the Spanish army. However, his martyrdom gave hope to the existing rebels and led them to fight stronger, regroup faster, and gain more recruits to fight the Spaniards. The new recruits were usually people from the rural areas of eastern Cuba. The Spanish army was losing the battle, and their control over the lands in eastern Cuba.

Most of the rebels lived with the ordinary population in the countryside, and as a result, the Spanish Army could not identify the rebels from the normal population, offering them a huge advantage. To overcome this issue, the head of the Spanish Army in Cuba, General Valeriano Weyler, decided to separate the so-called *good* from the *bad* (the rebels). Weyler's strategy was to force the so-called good *campesinos*[6] into the Cuban cities with the hope of leaving the rebels in the countryside. In other words, Weyler created concentration camps of farmers and villagers in the cities that not only caused overpopulation but also starvation (Cuba: A New History, 2005). The rapid decline of food production caused the economy to collapse. As a result of the high death rate in the concentration camps, *La Necrópolis de Cristóbal Colón*[7] did not have sufficient space to accommodate the high number of new deaths. Consequently, the families who already had their dead buried had to pay a maintenance fee of $10 every five years. People with no money who were affected by the economic crisis had to accept the fact that their dead had to be dug up. Given the economic crisis and the fact that many people could not afford to pay $10 to keep their dead buried, the graves were dug up, and the skulls and bones of the dead were thrown to the side and piled up, forming a huge hill. There are still horrific photos available of the "boneyards" in Havana's Colón Cemetery displaying a boneyard of human skull and bones (Figure 2). In 1896, during the horrible situation that Weyler had created in Cuba, around 200,000 out of 1.9 million people lost their lives (Lawrence, 2015).

U.S. newspapers published photos of the horrific situation in Cuba. The papers were sided with the revolutionaries and exposed the atrocities committed by the Spaniards. This awareness provoked calls for the U.S. to

---

[6] Farmers.
[7] The Colón Cemetery in Havana.

intervene in Cuba. The U.S. never intervened directly, but instead sent one of its warships to the port of Havana to protect American interests and businesses. This American ship (USS Maine ACR-1) was later blown to pieces in the Havana harbor. This is the event that caused the U.S. to declare war on Spain in 1898 with a mandate to free Cuba and help the Cubans achieve their independence.

Figure 2. Havana's Colón Cemetery Boneyard in 1899.

As history tells us, the Americans won the war and helped Cuba attain its independence. Cuba, however, did not become fully independent at that time but was considered a protectorate of the United States. During the protectorate era, many American companies had taken up a noticeable part of the Cuban economy. Furthermore, the U.S. Army was still present in Cuba, a presence that shattered any dreams of independence. The Cuban people had a vision of being independent and fought hard to achieve their independence from Spain with the help of the Americans. Still, they went from being a colony of Spain to being entirely dependent on the U.S. The Cuban people felt that they got out of the frying pan but into the fire.

If you have been to Cuba, you might have noticed that Cuban's refer to the farmers as *Guajiros*. Although this word refers to the indigenous Wayuu people in modern day Colombia, the history of this word in Cuba dates back to when the American soldiers helped the Cubans in their fight against the Spaniards. The Americans used to call the farmers who were fighting the Spaniards "war heroes." Over time, this word changed to *guajiros*, which perhaps was a mispronunciation of the phrase "war heroes." To celebrate the triumph of the war against the Spaniards, Cubans and Americans celebrated this victory with a drink that is made up of Coca-Cola and rum. The Americans brought Coca-Cola to the island, while rum was produced locally from sugar cane. Symbolically, as the Americans and Cubans came together to defeat the Spaniards, a product of each country came together to create a refreshing drink called "Cuba Libre," which fittingly, means "Free Cuba" in Spanish.

To end the war as well as the occupation, the U.S. and Cuba reached a deal so that Cuba could attain its independence, while simultaneously allowing the U.S. to protect its assets, properties, and other interests. This agreement, which passed on March 2, 1901, is known famously as the Platt Amendment. One year after the Platt Amendment, and as part of the deal of independence, Cuba authorized the U.S. to have a military base in Cuba, and hence the U.S. established Guantanamo base, carrying a rent of $4,085 per year. This rent was actually to be paid in $2,000 gold coins, but the decoupling of the U.S. dollar from the Gold standard caused this discrepancy (Strauss, 2009).

The U.S. influence on Cuban public affairs, as well as the Cuban economy, continued until the end of Fulgencio Batista's presidency in 1959. During Batista's presidency, the gap between the rich and the poor in Cuba had grown vast; most of the sugar industry was controlled by U.S. interests with minor involvement of the Cuban people (except for wealthy sugar landowners). Havana had become the gambling and prostitution capital of Latin America.

In the "party town" of the Caribbean, anything could happen. There were brothels and casinos across Havana, along with easy access to cocaine and any other drugs you could think of. Casino and nightclub licenses were easily granted if you had the minimum required money to invest. However, the business of brothels and casinos was mainly controlled by U.S. organized crime. According to some reports, Batista was also the beneficiary of the profit of some of these operations (Capeci, 2004).

U.S. private enterprises controlled the majority of Cuba's wealth, which included assets like mines, land, and hotels. There was an illuminating difference between the rich Havana and the poor countryside, the latter a place that did not have running water, where people were stuck in perpetual debt, unemployment, hunger, and lack of equal access to medical care.

A Cuban friend once told me that during the Batista era, in the eastern city of Las Tunas, there was only one hospital that was designated to service the surrounding towns. In other words, if you were living in Las Parras (a village near Las Tunas), you would have to travel long distances to the township of Las Tunas just to have a doctor check you out. The main issue at the time was that the people neither had the money to travel to Las Tunas nor the money to pay for the medical bills. Medical services, education, and housing were not available for everyone, and this was all happening at a time when Cuba was largely considered to be one of the most prosperous countries in Latin America. Investment capital and the circulation of money in the Cuban economy had increased Cuba's Gross Domestic Product (GDP) to a level equal to that of some European countries. However, the gap between the rich and the poor was large and very evident. This gap widened as one moved from the western provinces of Cuba towards the eastern provinces.

Unemployment, poverty, social injustice, government corruption were rampant while the wealth of the country was enjoyed by Batista's circles and foreign stakeholders.

This led to the dissatisfaction of the people and to the organization of university student uprisings in Havana and Santiago de Cuba. Batista dealt with the uprisings by raiding the activists' homes, torturing and then executing the factions who were against his government. The executions were at times conducted in public to create fear amongst the populous. This atmosphere of inequality and repression planted the seeds for a change, triggering a series of events that culminated with the Cuban revolution of 1959.

The Cuban revolution had both domestic and international repercussions. It is, however, important to think about the reasons for the revolution as well as its purpose. In other words, what was the vision set out as a result of the revolution? What were the objectives of the revolution? Did it reach its intended goals of creating a higher quality of life and a democratic society for the Cuban people?

The Cuban people had always yearned for their independence and always sought to decide their affairs. To achieve their freedom, Cubans needed to manage everyone's expectations and make deals with all interested parties, which in this case were the Spaniards and the Americans. Furthermore, managing the expectations of the interested foreign parties entailed sharpening their political skills and looking for ways to survive. Cuba is a small nation in comparison to Spain or the U.S., and to remain independent, it had to learn how to negotiate and play politics with many countries who were interested in impacting its independence. Consequently, survival is a skill that the Cubans are very adept at.

Summarizing Cuban history is important to emphasize that today's Cuba is a result of what happened in the past. The fight for independence and the results of both good and bad decisions had an impact on why this country is how it is today. This historical background will help you frame the Cuban revolution. The Cuban people had been under pressure and had suffered injustice from the moment

Christopher Columbus set foot on the island. Nevertheless, they resisted the pressure and fought for independence. They hoped for a brighter future then, and they still do today.

CHAPTER IV: *LA SOCIEDAD CUBANA DE HOY* – CUBAN SOCIETY TODAY

"Qué triste es recoger cosechas de espinas y amarguras, cuando se siembra abrigando la esperanza de recoger flores y aplausos".

"How sad it is to harvest crops of thorns and bitterness, when you sow with the hope of collecting flowers and applause."

Máximo Gómez

Cuba shows a lot of promise as a tourist destination. There is an omnipresent sound of upbeat people salsa dancing, and it is home to arguably the most exotic beaches in the Caribbean. Cuba also boasts having the safest streets in Latin America, and well-educated people. Refreshing Daiquiris, Piña Coladas, and the famous Mojitos help as well. The local people are also part of what makes it promising, as they are generally friendly and helpful. The fact that Cuba has one of the highest literacy rates in Latin America means that there are few barriers to striking a meaningful conversation with the locals about any topic you wish. In short, Cuba has a lot to offer a traveler looking for relaxation and adventure alike.

Perhaps the perception of the average tourist is that in Cuba, everything is available for Cubans as it is for the tourists. The tourist's perception may be that even though the way of life is different, it is not that off from how things function in the rest of the world. To an average tourist visiting the usual spots, all the necessities seem to be available in the stores, restaurants, hotels, and bars, and the prices are relatively low compared to those in Canada and the U.S. For example, if you run out of shampoo, you can go to a store in the city and buy an imported bottle of shampoo for about the same price that you would typically pay in Toronto or New York. The same story goes with a toothbrush, deodorant, and other essential personal necessities, with the only difference being that you would not find the same variety that is available in North American stores. Also, if you want to cook your meal in a *Casa Particular* (rental houses authorized by the government for tourists), you can pay the same price as what you would pay for chicken or vegetables back home. Interestingly, beef is borderline illegal in Cuba but is offered at resorts. I'll expand upon that later.

Taxis are around 50% cheaper in comparison to what you would pay in large cities in North America. For example, at the time of writing this book in 2020, one could take a taxi from Pinar Del Río (the far western part of Cuba) to the city of Baracoa (in the far east), which is a distance of 1,150 km (or 714 miles) for only about $650 CUC.[8] The distance is roughly the same from Washington D.C. to Miami, Florida, but the same fare by taxi or Uber in the U.S. will cost you more than $1,500. As a tourist, one might expect that your average Cuban has access to all of the essential food commodities and the potential to purchase and carry a lifestyle that is 50% cheaper than what it would cost the average North American. That was my assumption

---

[8] As of January 1st, 2021, Cuba began using a single currency (the CUP, or *moneda nacional*) after decades of operating under a system of dual currencies which the government believed was more advantageous to the Cuban economy. For purposes of clarity in this book, all monetary references are approximate and in U.S. dollars.

as well, an assumption that turned out to be far from the truth.

Cuba follows a state-controlled and state-planned economy where the government is the largest business owner and the largest employer in the country, following in the footsteps of the socio-economic model of the old Soviet Union. However, since 2010, this model has drastically evolved from its original form and has improved to allow for private ownership, licenses for small businesses, greater autonomy of government enterprises, and many other reforms that I will elaborate on later in the book. The consequences of the state-run economy have been a narrow band of fixed wages for employees. Below were the average monthly salaries before the reunification of the two currencies (based on multiple sources in Cuba):

- Factory Worker: $16
- Babysitter: $10
- Family Doctor: $48
- Specialist Doctor: $68
- Singer at your favorite resort: $80 at the high end.

After the reunification of the two currencies in January 2021, the Cuban government increased the minimum salary to 2100 pesos or $87.5 given an official exchange rate of 24 pesos to one dollar. The value of the CUP on the black market is close to 50 pesos to the U.S. dollar while the price of goods has increased significantly. Consequently, even though the salaries were raised, in reality, the purchasing power of the Cuban people remains close to $42 per month.

Now, if a short taxi ride costs $10, a sandwich costs $3, dinner for one at a restaurant costs $15, and a shampoo costs $7, then you may wonder how one could survive on an average salary of $42 per month?

Imagine your salary is $5,000 per month and that a bottle of shampoo costs $2,000, a short taxi ride costs $3,000, and going to a restaurant is going to cost you $10,000. What would you do and how would you survive? The answer to this question impacts Cubans every day, causing them to have grave concern about their future, their lifestyle, and to make tough decisions in regard to the quality of the products they use, their food and nutrition, transportation, relationships, entertainment, and more.

Because of the state-controlled economy, the government subsidizes food and housing for its citizens. For example, every Cuban has a food booklet, *La Libreta*, that has a list of items that can be purchased every month for meager prices at the government's convenience stores or *Bodegas*. The list is a lengthy one, but only four or five items are generally available at the government store. At the start of every month, there are huge lines to buy the items in these food booklets, and when it's someone's turn, some of the items may already be gone.

Even if you're one of the lucky ones, these food subsidies do not meet the demand of a single person, much less an entire family. To give you an idea, here is what the *Libreta* allocates for one person:

- Small bread – One for every day of the month
- Rice – 5 lbs. per month
- Grains (beans) – 8 ounces
- Chicken – 6 ounces (every 15 days)
- Picadillo de Soya (textured soy protein) – 6 ounces
- Eggs – 5 eggs per month at a discount and 5 more at a slightly higher price per month
- Cooking oil – 8 ounces per month
- Sugar – 4 lb per month
- Mortadella – 8 ounces per person
- Compote – 7 mini cans (only for babies up to 3 years of age)
- Salt – One small packet
- Coffee – 1 coffee packet per month

- Matches
- Milk (powdered, not liquid) – allowed only if you have kids under 7 years old or if you are a senior citizen

Items that do not usually appear in the *Libreta* stores are:

- Fish – never available even though Cuba is surrounded by the ocean
- Beef[9] – very rarely available (every 3 to 4 months) for small children under 7 years of age

The items outside of the above list are not subsidized, and people have no option but to purchase the rest of the necessities in the *Tiendas en Divisas,* also known as the currency stores. The currency stores often have more supply, more variety, and higher quality products, which are imported by the Cuban government to cater to the tourists. In other words, the Cuban government uses dollars or hard currencies to import goods and sells these goods in dollars. If you need shoes, a dress, or a shirt, you would need to purchase these items at the currency store, and you would have to pay in dollars for the items. Since the government only imports certain brands and specific sizes, you may not even find your size. Even though you may have saved for a year to buy a pair of shoes, you may be out of luck and have to settle for a size that does not fit you or be forced to forgo the purchase. The other sad news is that, as a customer, you have to pay even more for a brand that may cost less in North America, as the Government needs to cover its transportation cost and make a little bit of money off the top of the imported items. The other reason why prices are higher in Cuba in comparison to the U.S. is that there is not enough supply and competition to lower the price while keeping the demand satisfied. In other words, the

---

[9] It is prohibited and illegal to kill a cow in Cuba without permission from the State.

Government does not purchase and import these items in bulk to achieve lower average costs per unit. The alternative is to buy clothes at a relatively lower price by purchasing directly from Cubans who often travel to other countries. Certain countries (at the time of writing this book in 2020) do not require a visa for Cubans. Russia, Trinidad & Tobago, Guyana, and Panama have recently relaxed these requirements. Cubans travel to these countries in order to purchase clothes in hopes of bringing them back to Cuba to sell to their family members or neighbors.

Having mentioned the income constraint that many Cubans face, one may wonder: how can Cubans afford to obtain a passport and buy a plane ticket? Just as it happens in the rest of the world, only those who can afford to travel do so. The difference is that Cubans often need to sell all of their belongings. Some may sell their jewelry, or they may have family abroad willing to provide the initial investment to import clothing.

Importers typically sell the clothing merchandise within their neighborhoods. Selling the imported merchandise often takes a long time because the neighborhood customers either don't have the money to buy and need to save up, or they might pay in monthly installments if they need to purchase the clothes right away. For example, if a pair of Converse shoes costs $40, a neighbor will provide the shoe under the condition that monthly installments are made over four months (i.e. $10 per month). Of course, there is generally no interest charged on the payment. Another method is sales from merchants who make handmade clothes and sell them in the city centers. These prices will also be in dollars. There are also international donations made by various churches and religious groups to Cuba. Interestingly enough, these don't always follow their intended path. I have heard from some Cubans that certain people who work within the government would resell these donations to the people through stores called *Trapichopis* (a store for used/recycled clothes) instead of providing them for free to the people. I cannot independently confirm whether this claim by folks in Cuba is true or false.

Now that the groundwork is laid in regard to goods, prices, and salaries, I will start to explore some of the challenges facing Cuba within various sectors of its economy.

Healthcare

Providing access to timely and high-quality medical services can be challenging at times, even though Cuba has a reputation for having a robust medical system. While the country offers healthcare for Cuban citizens and permanent residents free of charge, the reality may not be as promising as it is perceived from the outside. Every major city has a main hospital where essential medical equipment, such as ultrasound machines, MRIs, etc., can be found, and each city has a *policlínico*.[10] Before the 1959 revolution, Cuba had the third-highest number of doctors per thousand inhabitants in Latin America (Gott, Cuba: A New History, 2005). This concentration of doctors was mostly in the prosperous occidental part of the country in the cities of Havana, Matanzas, and Santa Clara. As I mentioned in Chapter 2, there was only one hospital in the city of Las Tunas to serve the needs of farmers and people in the area. During that time, folks from farms far away from the city of Las Tunas would journey there because there were no medical facilities and no doctors in their villages. The journey from the nearby farms was undoubtedly expensive, as was the hospital visit. If you didn't have the cash, you would not get the treatment. As a result, the availability of doctors in the rural area of the Oriental provinces was low due to the lack of attention paid by the central government towards the eastern regions, which unfortunately continues to this day. The eastern provinces of Cuba still do not get

---

[10] Health clinic.

the proper attention they deserve, and, as described in Chapter 3, this lack of attention has gone on since the ruling of the Spaniards.

After the revolution, Cuba worked towards providing a universal free healthcare system to its citizens and began to significantly increase the number of doctors per capita, thanks to free university tuition and through extensive training of doctors. Today, Cuba has continued to focus on healthcare, seeing significant achievements in its healthcare system. Those include the eradication of many infectious diseases through universal vaccinations, production of medical drugs (including antiretroviral drugs, which are provided at lower costs for HIV patients), elimination of transmission of HIV from mother to child, the lowest transmission of HIV in the Western Hemisphere, and the proper handling of the COVID-19 pandemic. Cuban doctors have even ventured to Africa, Latin America, and the Caribbean to put their skills to work. In 2020, Cuban doctors traveled to the COVID-19 hot zones of Italy, South Africa, Jamaica and Perú to lend a hand.

Aside from the moral benefits, the international participation of Cuban doctors has resulted in a significant contribution to Cuba's GDP and an increased availability of hard currency for Cuba. The net gain from sending Cuban doctors abroad has brought in more money for Cuba than the export of nickel did, and the revenue was almost in par with that of the tourism industry (Gary Clyde Hufbauer, 2014).

Although Cuban doctors have become a solid export for the country, the international mission for Cuban doctors has not been an easy one. However, the incentives are there, as these doctors opt for accepting the contracts because they are given a higher salary in hard currency (ranging from $500 to $1,400 USD per month, depending on the country). The high salary of doctors who work abroad constitutes typically 20% to 25% of the salary paid by the host country to the Cuban government. For example, in 2018, the Brazilian government paid a monthly salary of $3,600 USD to the Cuban government for every doctor it hosted. However, doctors would typically only be paid $1,000 USD per month while doing their work in Brazil (NUGENT, 2018). Even then, this represents an incredibly large lift compared to the wages the doctors receive at home. Another perk that comes with accepting a foreign medical mission contract is that the doctors can often bring back well-needed appliances, automobiles, and other items that are not available in Cuba, free of tariffs.

However, once at their international workplace, the doctors are limited in their freedom of movement and are often watched and told what they need to do. They are also not allowed to bring their families with them. Another downside is that if a doctor is pregnant, they are forced to go back to Cuba to give birth, as the Cuban government wants to prevent the newborn child from obtaining foreign citizenship (NUGENT, How Doctors Became Cuba's Biggest Export, 2018).

The international missions of Cuban doctors also have many domestic impacts. Since Cuba sends a lot of its best physicians abroad, there is often a shortage of experienced practitioners who can provide a high quality of service to the people in Cuban hospitals and medical clinics. In other words, there is a serious brain drain issue. The remaining doctors in Cuba either lack experience or are interns. Of course, for the tourists or political and military elites, experienced physicians are still available in the best hospitals across the country. In essence, Cuba has a hidden double healthcare system, with one side catering to the tourists and elites with highly experienced doctors, and the other one caring for people who often are denied access to fast and high-quality treatment. Unfortunately, if you don't have an inside connection to a doctor who is either your neighbor or a friend, or if you don't bring them a gift, you will not get the priority you deserve and most likely will need to wait in line for a long time to get medical attention (Sergio Díaz-

Briquets, 2006).

It is an uncomfortable truth that almost anything in the medical system can be resolved with a bit of cash. For example, if you want to give birth without seven or more interns watching you or if you would like to choose a C-section or epidural instead of natural birth, your money could go a long way towards influencing that decision by the doctors. It's not only the preferential treatment that can be influenced, however. Due to the lack of availability of essential medical supplies, doctors sometimes have no choice but to reuse medical gloves. Sometimes there are no anesthetics available to be used during tooth removals, and in this case, a bit of money can save you a lot of pain.

I think back to the time I had to accompany my friend who was experiencing severe stomach pain due to gastritis to the Hospital Clínico Quirúrgico Holguín.[11] I suspect that his gastritis was most likely caused by the lack of proper nutrition in Cuba. Regardless, the conditions that I saw first-hand paled in comparison to Canadian hospitals and were horrendously sub-optimal from a sanitation perspective. I saw floors with vomit, a lack of privacy as patients were on different beds side by side without a separator, unflushed feces in the toilets, and the smell of formaldehyde, which was nausea-inducing. Even when my friend returned the next day to the hospital for his follow-up appointment, he mentioned to me that the vomit from the night before was still on the floor.

There have been many cases where patients were not treated correctly in the Cuban medical system. There have been cases where one patient was infected with Hepatitis C due to improper sterilization of the needles during blood tests (Rosen, 2016: Hepatitis may be linked to injections in Cuba, 1991). Another case was in regard to a prostate exam given to a senior citizen who was considered a *caso social*, which translates to social case, meaning homeless, or

---

[11] Holguín Surgical and Clinical Hospital.

extremely poor with typically no family. The doctor had to perform a prostate exam on the gentleman but in front of seven young interns. The procedure had to be done with soap and water used as a lubricant because neither lubricants nor gloves were available. The procedure was a bit complicated without the gloves and sufficient lubricant, which resulted in laughter from fellow students, demeaning the gentleman, and violating his right to privacy. These are just a few examples which show the severe problems that lie at the core of Cuba's medical system: lack of essential medical supplies, causing the re-use of medical gloves and face masks, lack of essential drugs at the pharmacies while anything can be found on the black market, and lack of infrastructure needed to get the doctor to the hospital in time for surgery. Often the doctors in smaller cities ride bicycles to work, and in some of the eastern provinces, you might see them taking a horse carriage.

Drugs are sometimes stolen by the employees and sold on the black market to make extra cash, as pharmacists' salaries do not pay to cover monthly family expenditures. The robbery of these essential drugs results in the unavailability of critical medication for cancer patients and the elderly at subsidized and affordable prices. A doctor's salary, even though it has been raised from $30 to $68 (depending on the type of specialist and their experience), simply does not incentivize doctors to provide a high-quality service. Therefore, some doctors accept gifts to get people ahead of the line. Even things like perks for the doctors, such as Christmas gifts or extra vacation, aren't readily offered.

There is also a lack of attention to the details from some of the doctors. In the Lenin Hospital in Holguín, there have been cases where the doctors have mistakenly misplaced the body of a person who recently passed away with an unconscious person who just came out of surgery. The corpse was taken on the stretcher to the recovery unit, while the patient who just came out of the operation was taken to the morgue. There are also cases of reported lack of moral consideration by some of the doctors. In November 2017, there was a fatal shark attack that led to the killing of a young 22-year-old man from Holguín in the coastal beach town of Guardalavaca. The pictures of the shark bites and injuries to the corpse of this young man were circulated on Cuban social media after his death. It turns out that the doctor broke the patient's confidentiality and shared the horrific photos of the body of this young man, which circulated on social media and ended up on practically everyone's phone in Cuba.

Many foreigners travel to Cuba for "medical tourism." If you pay *en divisa* (American dollars, or hard currency), then you will receive the best medical service with everything (ranging from latex gloves to MRI machines) available to you just because you paid in dollars. However, for the ordinary citizens who make the average monthly salary, they have to know someone in the medical system or take a lovely gift (sometimes cash) for the doctor or the nurse in order to get priority service and not wait in line. A small gift will always help if you are going for a blood test. At times, the laboratory may take your blood and may call you back again after a week because the reactive agent to detect abnormalities in your blood might not have been available. However, often with a bit of *dinero,*[12] you will be prioritized accordingly, and your blood will find its necessary reactive agent, so you don't have to be called twice to give blood.

I am in no way attempting to negate the great work that the majority of the true Cuban doctors, nurses, and medical staff do day in and day out, working with honor and integrity. But, unfortunately, the problem of making ends meet affects one of the building blocks of society: the healthcare system.

---

[12] Money.

Food and General Services

As mentioned earlier, covering basic necessities in Cuba is a daily challenge, as the monthly food allowance that is given at the *bodegas*, or government stores, does not meet the needs of Cuban families. At the same time, the low monthly wages do not allow for people to buy meat, poultry, seafood, and vegetables at the *tienda en divisa*, or currency grocery stores. Even if the people had the money, many of the items do not appear in the currency stores.

For example, vegetables filled with antioxidants such as lettuce, tomatoes, and any plant-based chlorophyll-filled food simply are not available in stores. While farmers sometimes bring fresh fruits and vegetables into the cities to sell, the prices are still too high and unaffordable for most. For the ones that are affordable, the quality of the product is not high because of the ripening, maturing agents that are usually added to them.

Because of the extremely high cost of getting around in Cuba in comparison to the wages, a person living in the city has to spend a significant portion of their monthly wages on transportation just to go outside the city to buy fruits and vegetables. Once at the farm, said person will then have to pay an additional half of their monthly salary to purchase the produce. As a result, it is challenging to obtain healthy vegetables and fruits year-round at a reasonable price.

The primary meat of choice for the Cuban people is pork, which is widely consumed and traditionally roasted during Christmas, New Year's Eve, and other festivities. Seafood is also common, as the most highly available seafood is the catfish or *claria*, which was introduced to Cuba from Africa to provide an alternate source of food post-collapse of the Soviet Union (PADGETT, 2019). It comes as no surprise that a country surrounded by the sea has a lot of seafood. What is odd is the prevalence of malnutrition while there is such a large amount of fish available around the island. Once again, the government controls the fishing industry. So, for example, a fisherman living in Gibara (a coastal fishing town in the province of Holguín) cannot fish in bulk to sell sea delicacies, such as shrimp, octopus (*pulpo*), or lobsters to the public. Because the government controls the fishing industry, there is a lack of competition, and ample inefficiencies in fishing operations, causing the prices of seafood to be higher than most Cubans can afford.

A lot of the families eat less, eat unhealthily, or are forced to go to bed hungry because of the lack of food available at a subsidized or cheaper price. Although a glaring problem, the Cuban government has not invested significant resources to solve this food crisis. The farms use outdated tools and machinery, and the harvesting is done manually by the *campesinos* or farmers. There has not been any significant investment in the farming industry to increase crop yield and conduct mass production to satisfy the population's food demand.

Beef is controlled by the state and can only be sold in government-controlled restaurants. It is illegal to kill a cow, and the prison sentence can be close to that of killing a human being in Cuba (Medina, 2013). The plants that are grown in Cuba, such as sugarcane, citrus, coffee, tobacco, plantains, yucas, and potatoes, are not able to satisfy the population's demand. The inefficient agricultural practices, high fuel and transportation costs, and a lack of available and reliable transportation infrastructure have led to urban farming practices in the cities. Many Cubans have hens and roosters in the backyards to use their eggs and meat whenever necessary, while some families raise pigs to either sell or consume their meat.

The inefficient agricultural system, reduced farm yields, high taxes on the private farms which constitute 80% of Cuba's food production, and lack of adequate investment in this industry have led to the importation of most food necessities by the government (Alvarez, 2019). Cuba imports between 60 and 70 percent of its food mainly in the form of grains, rice, chicken, and, most importantly, powdered milk for a price tag of $2 billion annually (Frank, 2017).

During the Trump administration, sanctions were placed on Venezuela's oil and shipping sectors transporting goods to Cuba. Consequently, the availability of food and the importation of essential items from Venezuela was severely impacted. The impacts of the sanctions on Venezuela in 2019 resulted in a shortage of food supply in Cuban dollarized or currency stores. The lack of food, in turn, created long line ups and general dissatisfaction and unrest amongst the people, as items such as chicken and other goods were not available at the bodegas or hard currency stores.

Cuba's agricultural problems are one of the greatest threats to its national security and are somewhat complex in nature. Their root causes will be further explored in the following chapters. However, Cuba has always depended indirectly on foreign powers for its food and energy production. The wakeup moment for Cuba came after the collapse of the Soviet Union, when it was forced to move towards independence in terms of food production. It's possible that the current problems could have been avoided if Cuba had focused on becoming self-sufficient earlier on, investing in the agricultural infrastructure to produce chicken, beef, and vegetables in large volumes, ultimately increasing the supply and lowering the price.

Tourism

The history of tourism in Cuba predates the revolution of 1959. Due to the geographical proximity to the continental U.S., as well as its tropical weather, pristine beaches, and UNESCO world heritage sites, Cuba has been an attractive market for tourism. Before the revolution, Havana was the hedonistic capital of the Caribbean and offered a wide array of casinos, drinks, nightlife, and brothels for tourists. Not all tourism was healthy, though, as Havana was a playground for gangsters, U.S. organized crime families, and the rich who could afford what Havana had to offer. Gambling and casinos were one of the primary sources of entertainment and revenue, followed by the oldest profession in the world: prostitution. One independent work estimates that over 11,000 prostitutes were working in Cuba's sex industry in over 270 brothels before the 1959 revolution (Rodriguez Garcia, Van Voss, & Van Nederveen Meerkerk, 2017).

After the revolution, there was a thorough cleanup of all casinos, brothels, and prostitution practices as the tourism industry, in general, declined post-revolution due to the U.S. embargo. Following the cleanup, during the Soviet era from the 60s to the 90s, there was not a high volume of tourists. However, that all changed with the collapse of the Soviet Union and the start of *El Período Especial*, or the Special Period, which lasted from 1991 to 2000. During the Special Period, economic support from the Eastern Bloc and the Soviet Union for Cuba disappeared, and due to the economic crisis in this period, Cuba was forced to come up with a way to turn its economic wheel. It was at this point that Cuba made the choice to open up its doors to tourism.

Since the 1990s, relaxed policies by the government towards the tourism sector, as well as joint partnerships with industry-leading international hotel brands, have opened ways for foreign companies to invest in Cuba's tourism industry. This industry boomed, especially in the resort town of Varadero, where new hotels were constructed to cater to the high volume of visitors, mainly from Canada. The close diplomatic relationship between Canada and Cuba provided the opportunity for many Canadian tourists to enjoy the year-round tropical weather of the island, with the only thing standing in the way being a 3h 20m flight from Toronto to Varadero. The diplomatic relationships between these countries were cordially maintained after the 1959 revolution. Canada did not follow America in cutting ties with Cuba, and as a result, Canadians constituted the highest number of tourists in Cuba, followed by European countries. That trend continues to this day, as Canadians bring the largest number of tourists to the island, followed by the United States (at the time of writing of this book) (Canada - Cuba Relations, 2018). After President Trump's election in the U.S., travel restrictions to the island were restored, so there has been a severe decline of U.S. tourism to the island. This decrease was exacerbated by the suspension of cruise ship entries to Cuba, which was the primary mode of transportation for American tourists visiting the island.

Nowadays, Cuba has one of the lowest rates of return for repeat tourists. This is due to the increasing prices of tourist activities and services offered in the country compared to other Caribbean destinations, poor customer service, low food quality, and a lack of adequate infrastructure for transportation. Most of the tourists who travel to Cuba stay at all-inclusive beachfront resorts and experience the bubble that I mentioned at the start of this book.

One is able to find different classes of hotels, from 1-star to 5-star. Although there are some exceptions, the quality of services in the average hotels is not on par with that of hotels in Mexico or the Dominican Republic. One of the biggest challenges impacting these hotels is the food quality (and variety), as well as the quality of customer service provided by staff members, bartenders, and waiters. Over the past few years, there has been a considerable emphasis by international brands like Meliá Hotels International, the Iberostar Group, Royalton Resorts, to name a few, on how the quality of service should be rendered by the staff and how the clients should be treated.

In the past, you might have gone to a restaurant in an all-inclusive resort, and the items on the menu would not be available. Furthermore, the overall quality of food would not have resulted in an overall appealing culinary experience. Sometimes, burger meat is mixed with ground pork, and this is not disclosed to folks who have dietary restrictions. At restaurants, waiters may not pay enough attention to their seated costumers, even though this is standard practice in the service industry. The quality of the drinks may not be as high as expected, while standard recipes are often not followed. For example, one of the many drinks that tourists love to try in Cuba is the mojito, which is considered Cuba's national drink. At some resorts, the mojito is often prepared with syrup because peppermint, which is the principal ingredient, is not available.

There are many other issues that I have come across or heard about that cause an overall bad experience. The experience that you may have depends mainly on the category of the hotel brand and on whether the hotel is newly constructed. Of course, these issues could also be a problem in other hotels around the world, but they seem to be frequent in Cuba.

I don't wish to make generalizations regarding the hard-working people in Cuba's tourism industry. However, it takes only one or two items to severely impact someone's vacation in a negative manner. After all, it would not be fair, and it would be undoubtedly illegal, to falsely advertise the hotel's star ratings and deceive tourists who have been anxiously anticipating and saving for their vacation.

During and post the Obama administration, in anticipation of the arrival of U.S. tourists, many existing and repeat tourists have chosen not to return to Cuba and have elected to turn to other destinations for their vacations. It is clear that there is a huge opportunity for tourism in Cuba, but the prices have to match the quality of the service being provided. In a day and age where you can fly anywhere in the world for less than you ever could, competition is fierce. As it stands now, Cuba has a lot of room for improvement to compete at the global stage in tourism. Let's take a deeper dive into this quality gap between the all-inclusive hotels in Cuba and their competitors.

In my opinion, the following factors impact the lack of

quality of service despite increased investment by the Cuban government in its tourism industry. The following factors are inevitably intertwined with Cuba's overall economic policies, and will be explored in detail:

- Inability to guarantee the necessary supplies to carry out day to day business
- Lack of motivation for employees/managers to excel at work
- Rewarding bad work or bad behavior of employees in the tourism industry
- Lack of policies to encourage returning customers

Inability to guarantee the necessary supplies to carry out day to day business:

In Cuba, it is challenging for a hotel to obtain the required material and food products that are needed to operate the business. For example, in regard to food products, the majority of the hotels in Cuba do not have an import license, and as a result, they are dictated by the Cuban government to buy their necessities from the official government suppliers (Press, 2018). The only issue with purchasing the products from government suppliers is that the price is higher than the products offered in the free market. In addition, even if the amount is adequate, the quality is not there, as the government may import only one or two items, which may not represent the quality standard advertised by the hotel. For example, if a 4 or 5-star hotel in Cayo Coco needs to buy olive oil, the hotel may not find the high-quality brand name that they would like to offer to the customers and are forced to pay a higher price for a lower quality olive oil. The low-quality olive oil may not be in line with what the hotel is advertising itself to be (in this case, a 5-star resort). Another issue might be the lack of a guarantee of the supply of olive oil. The government may import a certain quantity of olive oil, and because of the increased demand from the other hotels, the government stores may run out of stock. Given the unavailability of supplies, the hotel still needs to maintain its commitments to its customers and serve olive oil or use it in its dishes. With a lack of supply at the government stores, this would be an impossible task. If you ever visited Cuba and the glass-filled tube beside your balsamic vinegar looked more like cooking oil than olive oil, this would be the reason.

Other examples are the inability to import Canada AAA (similar to USDA Prime) meat or an adequate type of meat so that the customers can have good steaks. The government should be giving more import licenses to the hotels so that they are able to import what they need for their business. As mentioned previously, Cuba was importing 70% of its food from other countries, which amounts to nearly $2 billion annually. However, there are restrictions for hotels seeking to import food, the reason being that the government does not want to lose "hard currency" for items that may not add essential value to the Cuban economy.

Cuba utilizes the tourism industry to make money in the form of hard currencies like the U.S. dollar, euro, Japanese yen, British pound, or the Canadian dollar. It then uses these hard currencies to trade with other nations. When you travel to Cuba, you will exchange any of the aforementioned currencies for Cuban Pesos (CUP), which is not an internationally traded currency and has no value outside the island. The Cuban government has pegged the value of CUP to the U.S. dollar. It will gauge the value of the peso against other currencies, such as the Canadian dollar (CAD), based on fluctuations of the U.S. dollar against other currencies. The Cuban government typically charges a high spread when exchanging your hard currency for the CUP. In other words, the Cuban government gets more of your dollars and gives you fewer of the worthless CUPs. Consequently, the exchange rate is one way that the government makes money from tourists.

Once the government obtains your hard currency through exchanging your money, it would then use the currency to purchase goods and commodities from the international markets. For example, Cuba uses Canadian dollars obtained from tourists to purchase heavy machinery and electrical and electronic equipment from Canada, and uses euros to import other goods from Spain or other European Union (EU) countries.

But, back to the original question. Why does Cuba not give out import licenses to all the hotels? The reason is that for the hotels to import Canada AAA meat, they need to exchange CUP to CAD at the Central Bank of Cuba and then use CAD to purchase steak from Canada. However, this means that the Canadian dollar reserve will be reduced at the account of the Central Bank of Cuba. The Canadian dollar used to buy steak could have been used to purchase other essential items aside from steaks for tourists, like asphalt to repair Cuba's roads. As a result, the import restriction by private enterprises impacts virtually everything, from getting parts for a broken air conditioner to buying construction material to renovate the hotel. From the perspective of the Cuban government, these imported items are simply not on the priority list, as the government prefers to give priority to resolving the power and food shortages across Cuba rather than satisfying the demands of the tourists. Now, you might ask: "I have paid top dollar for this hotel, and I deserve the service." You are 100% right. The issue here is that the government should prioritize certain items in the tourism industry. After all, if the government is running and controlling the tourism business, then it is responsible for running it competitively, responsibly, and efficiently. Furthermore, as we will explore in Chapter 5, Cuba can invest in infrastructure to produce quality products (in this case, quality steak) on a domestic level and at lower prices than those in the international free market. Internal production at lower prices could reduce food imports and prevent the disappearance of Cuba's hard currency reserves.

Limitations within the tourism industry have resulted in significant overhead in everyday operations. There is a direct correlation between the economic challenges and the quality of the hotels. As a result, the operational overhead has led to a discrepancy between services advertised to the customers versus the services actually rendered.

Lack of motivation for employees/managers to excel at work:

There are many motivational theories, from reinforcement theory to the cognitive evaluation theory to my personal favorite, Vroom's Expectancy theory of motivation (Vroom, 1964). Expectancy Theory states that, for a person to be motivated, he or she must meet the following conditions in order:

1) The person believes that his or her actions and efforts will result in the attainment of the desired outcome. In other words, you expect or believe that you are capable of doing the task at hand, and if you put in the effort, you will achieve the results. For our discussion, this might look like a Cuban hotel employee asking themselves if they are capable of doing their job with outstanding quality.

2) The person believes that some kind of reward will be received if the person carries out the task. For that same Cuban employee, this might look like asking themselves "If I do my job correctly, would I get rewarded by the management with a higher salary and bonuses?"

3) The person values the reward that he or she is going to receive. In our example, this might look like an employee asking themselves if an increase in salary of $42 per month to $50 per month is worth it.

In some Cuban hotels, one may encounter employees

that may be indifferent to the customers' requests or may come across, by North American standards, as rude. Amongst the many reviews written on popular travel sites like Tripadvisor, the negative reviews often share the same sentiment from the hotel clients: the service was not up to par with what the tourists had expected it to be. Generally, negative reviews are complaints about the quality of services at the hotels. Referring to Vroom's theory, the services are rendered by the hotel employees who either do not see the light of the rewards at the end of the tunnel (Rule #2) or do not value that reward (Rule #3).

What leads to this presumed motivational crisis of employees? Is this the root cause of the lack of quality of services at hotels? As mentioned earlier, the inflation-adjusted average salary in Cuba is anywhere between $42 and $65, depending on the profession. At the same time, the cost of food (outside of the *bodegas*) is much higher than what the average national salary can cover.

However, even though tourism's salary lies within these limits, Cubans strive to secure a job in the tourism industry. This popularity arises from the fact that on top of the average monthly salary, a career in the tourism industry provides an opportunity to make tips in dollars. For bartenders, the daily tips per individual in a popular hotel in Varadero could be equivalent to the employee's monthly salary.

It is a known fact amongst Cubans that to have an expedited service, the clients would have to give a little more to receive a better service. What would you do if you were planning your anniversary dinner and there was no availability at the restaurant located in the all-inclusive hotel you had paid for? At the reservation desk, a $5 tip could go a long way in this situation. You don't want to wait at a bar to get a drink? No problem. Tip the bartender well, and he or she will take care of you. This may not seem any different from receiving high quality services in different parts of the world. The fundamental difference is that in Cuba, if you don't tip, you may not receive even the basic services. According to the Expectancy Theory of motivation, the three requirements are fulfilled because even though the employee's salary is not raised, the tip is great, and the employees seem to value this reward.

Tourism employees oftentimes hold professional degrees in engineering, law, or accounting, to name a few. However, these employees, in their professions, would not make enough given the low average monthly wage. Thus, those who went to school to work in these high-skilled jobs find themselves shifting gears and going into the tourism industry. With extensive professional training and the ability to speak English, these employees get hired right away as servers, bartenders, janitors, security guards, etc. With their credentials, these professionals do not even prefer to get promoted to managerial positions in the tourism industry because they end up making the average salary, not making the tips, and also would be obligated to have more responsibility. Based on the conversations that I have had with many tourism industry employees across various provinces in Cuba, the employees do not feel fulfilled in their jobs because they are not using the degrees they went to school for. But still, they stay.

Another thing to consider is that the brand name hotels have high expectations from their employees and set work quality standards similar to what you would find in North America and Europe. As a result, the average Cuban employee has to work within the framework of higher international standards. What happens to the salary then? Do foreign hotel companies pay more for adhering to higher international standards? The answer is yes. However, the employees still get paid the average monthly salary. The reality is that the top foreign hotel brand names will pay roughly $300 USD for each employee to the Cuban government, but the government will only pay just above the average salary to the employee, pocketing the rest. The average worker actually costs hotels such as the Meliá around $900 USD, which includes wages, taxes, bonuses, and benefits (Feinberg, 2016). The average Cuban tourism employee costs more to the hotels in comparison to that of a Dominican worker. However, the average Cuban tourism employee takes a smaller salary home.

Because of the competitive compensation policy present in the hotel industry in the Western world, foreign managers and employees working in Cuba are paid in the thousands of dollars per month. However, the hotel managers from the Cuban side who do the same work as the foreign managers will only get paid slightly above the average Cuban salary. Given these situations, the third point from Vroom's expectancy theory is not met, and there is no motivation to adhere to higher standards or try to do a great job, even at the managerial level.

Another distressing situation is that some employees cannot sustain the family expenses even by working in the tourism industry because, in the post-President Obama era, the number of U.S. tourists has been reduced significantly, followed by a reduction in tips. Some of the hotel employees are temporarily laid off to minimize hotel expenses during the slow tourism season, which is typically between May and October. The lucky ones who continue to work find it difficult to feed their families with the virtually nonexistent tips, average salary, and rising costs of necessities due to U.S. sanctions. Certain employees have told me that they needed to steal food, including chicken, often stuffing it in their clothes to take home to feed their families. At the police checkpoints, the officers usually check inside the employee buses for any suspicious or anti-revolutionary activities. A hotel employee shared one of his stories with me. During one of the inspections, the employee was nearly caught with stolen food in his backpack. Not only did he have food in his bag, but he had chicken attached to his body. He mentioned that he would not care so much about losing his job but rather the opportunities (tips and stolen food) that he has access to through his job to continue feeding his family.

In most of the all-inclusive hotels, the fridge in every room is usually stocked with beers and other beverages. Some employees resort to stealing and selling the daily beers the hotels give away for free to the tourists. Every day, the hotel staff will check the fridge, and if the guests consume the drinks, then they will provide the guests with more beers. However, if you happened not to have consumed your beers or your TuKola (the Cuban version of Coca-Cola), then the hotel staff will take home the daily beer allowance intended for tourist consumption. The stolen beers from the hotel inventory will have gone undetected because the hotel assumes that the guest drank the beer. The stolen beer will then be sold on the black market for a slightly lower price than the price the government sets nationally or will simply be consumed by the employee's family.

Another instance of theft is that of hotel employees using family members, neighbors, or friends who are guests at the same all-inclusive hotel to mule certain products out. The neighbor might order bottles of sparkling wine or other drinks that would be delivered to the room. They would then pack these items in their suitcases and would leave the hotel without being caught at police checkpoints. In return for the favor, the neighbor would get a couple of bottles as a gift, while the rest would be sold or consumed by the hotel employee.

Other tactics include those of bartenders at 5-star hotels who, when selling premium drinks (that are not included in the all-inclusive package) to their clients, do not fill the glasses with the full shot volume. So, if someone was to buy two shots of Santiago 20 year rum, the bartender may only pour you 1.75 shots but charge you for two. In other words: a bottle is divided into 25 shots and the employee has sold all 25 shots on paper, but in reality, he has poured the clients 22 shots, and the remaining three shots would be considered free leftovers. The repetition of this process would eventually accumulate the unsold portion of the bottle until a full bottle could be obtained free and clear. The bartenders will then sell the entire bottle at a discount to the tourists (under the table) who can trust not to rat them out. For example, a bottle of Havana Club 15 years, which is sold at a national fixed price of $150, is often sold about half that price to the tourists under the table.

Employees seem to draw their motivation from these side businesses rather than from promotions and perks. These employees run their mini businesses often without fear of losing their jobs, as the pain of losing their jobs simply does not amount to the pleasure of making money from stealing hotel products.

The information provided is based on my private interviews with employees and their managers that work in tourism. Of course, this does not apply to everyone. There are excellent employees and hard-working men and women in the tourism industry who go out of their way to make a difference despite the economic and social challenges they face daily. Many employees in the tourism industry work with honor and dignity and are against the wrongdoing of others. Moreover, these honorable employees are against those who choose to steal from the hotels under the justification and pretext that they are struggling to feed their families or that they are inventive by having a side business. The employees who steal often justify their actions by suggesting that the government takes from them. I do not deny the economic pressures at all, and perhaps an employee or two needed to steal so that their wives and kids didn't go hungry at night. I seek to only explore the root causes that create the current business and economic climate. These ideas will be explored further in Chapter 5, where we'll take a deep dive into the *Bloqueo* or Embargo.

Rewarding bad work or bad behavior of employees in the tourism industry:

When a customer complaint is brought forth, the hotel staff

will often correct the problem to avoid further escalation to their respective managers. However, there have been many cases where complaints have not yielded any results. While a manager may address complaints with an employee if they become repeat offenders, there are no real concrete measures that can be taken against the employee. In other words, it is very difficult to fire a hotel employee, and therefore, there is no fear of reprimand amongst the employees. As discussed earlier, employees are not afraid of losing their jobs, but instead are scared of losing the opportunity to make tips.

Because of the lack of concrete consequences of not doing a good job, there is no incentive for the employee not to keep making the same mistakes, so the system does not confront bad behavior, but rather, to some extent, rewards it. The incentive to be promoted seems to work negatively because the employees would rather not get promoted to the managerial level or to an office job position, since they would have to accept more responsibilities but with marginal pay increases.

Resorts in Cuba that are managed by international companies, often have two directors. One director will be Cuban, while the other is a foreign director from the international company. Even though there are many distinct responsibilities between the directors, many of the responsibilities overlap. In other words, the two directors have the same level of duties, with the only difference being that the Cuban director receives a salary of around $100 per month, while their counterpart from the foreign side gets a minimum of $5,000 monthly. There is no incentive to work harder or smarter for the Cuban director, as the expectations and level of responsibility are the same as the foreign director. Still, the difference in salaries is vast.

Lack of policies to encourage returning customers:

Over the past two decades, Cuba has funneled investment

in the tourism sector by building its tourism infrastructure, training staff, and partnering with international hotel management companies. The partnership with foreign companies, specifically those from Spain, Canada, and France, has brought the experience of hotel management, customer care, entertainment, and procurement of products to bring Cuban tourism up to par with that of its competition in the Dominican Republic, Jamaica, and Mexico. Although there are different tourism products catered to various niche markets, most Canadian tourists, which constitute over 30% of all the visitors to Cuba, prefer to stay at all-inclusive resorts.

Vacationing in Cuba looked a lot different during the pre-Obama years versus how it looked after President Obama left office. In the past, one could get a weeklong vacation at one of the best beaches for between $550 to $1200 CAD, including flight and hotel. Tourists were generally happy with their experience because the prices were so low, so their expectations were low to match. With the anticipation of American tourists flocking to the island, prices began to gradually rise. It seemed like a common occurrence that multimillion-dollar hotel construction projects would pop up in Havana, Varadero, Cayo Santa María, and Ramón de Antilla. However, the number of U.S. tourists anticipated was severely overestimated, as President Trump reversed some of President Obama's policies towards Cuba. This policy reversal also coincided with increased sanctions due to the Havana Syndrome that affected both Canadian and U.S. diplomatic staff, impacting the diplomats' hearing abilities. Other post-Obama policy reversals that had a negative impact include the sanctions on Venezuela that caused fuel and food shortages in Cuba, and the banning of cruise ships from docking at Havana's port, which prevented millions of Americans from visiting the island (Sarah Marsh, 2019).

The situation has caused a slowdown of the Cuban economy, particularly impacting the tourism sector. The loyal and repeat Canadian customers no longer have the same incentives to travel to Cuba because vacation prices are almost on par with those of Mexico, Dominican Republic, and Jamaica, but with lower quality of service and food and beverage.

Another reason is that the CAD to CUP conversion is not favorable for Canadian tourists due to reduced purchasing power, making Cuba an expensive and infeasible destination. Unfortunately, the authorities in Cuba have neither addressed the currency conversion issue to make it more favorable for their largest tourist customers, nor have they taken corrective measures to improve the quality of food and services at the hotels. The Cuban government cannot afford to change or devaluate the CUP because this would result in a lower hard currency reserve in Cuba's central bank, which Cuba badly needs to keep its ailing economy afloat.

Something else to consider as a factor is the difference in the way Cuban citizens are treated versus foreigners. I have many Canadian friends who have experienced delays at hotel check-ins and did not receive the same level of treatment once they stayed at the hotels with their Cuban significant other. When a Cuban national checks into a hotel with a foreign citizen, the Cuban government, through its security apparatus system, conducts a background check. The ID card of Cuban nationals is used to confirm if the Cuban national has previously been registered with other foreigners in different hotels or *casas particulares*. Furthermore, the hotel reception typically submits the data of the Cuban national to a security center, who in turn gives the Cuban national the right to enter the hotel or not. This system is supposedly implemented to prevent prostitution and to ensure that Cuban nationals do not end up with multiple foreigners. This system is not applied if two Cuban persons want to check-in together or if a Cuban person has been registered with other Cuban nationals. Hence, there is a double standard that does not address the core issue of prostitution in Cuba, but instead causes delays and degradation of service for couples who are not engaged in the act of prostitution.

Another common complaint from Cuban-foreign couples is that the Cuban government security personnel who are stationed at the hotels will sometimes privately approach the workers, bartenders, and maids regarding a Cuban national client. Women are typically investigated more than men. The security personnel will typically ask the staff if they have seen the Cuban guest with other foreigners before. With security personnel dressed in casual attire, it is hard to distinguish them from regular guests at the hotel. They aim to control prostitution, but in reality, they seem to be creating mistrust and a lack of privacy. I know this because one of my friends saw first-hand how security approached a bartender who happened to be the neighbor of my friend's spouse. Another friend told me the story of how one of their family members installed security cameras at the hotels and, according to him, there were previous cases where Cuban security personnel had installed hidden cameras in hotel rooms to monitor guests' activities. Although I cannot independently verify this claim, if accurate, this would be a clear violation of international privacy acts and hotel policies.

Another first-hand account from a friend is the practice of checking the suitcases of foreigners when they are not in the room. Apparently, as part of granting a rental license for *casas particulares*, the tourism department arranges mini-training sessions for the property owners, and during the training sessions, the property owner is suggested to search the guests' rooms. In other words, the owners of the rental places are expected to enter their guests' rooms, open their suitcases, and see if there are any suspicious items. They are even told to check the garbage cans. He concluded, and I quote: "¡Imagínense que tienen un enemigo en su casa!"[13]

---

[13] Imagine that you have an enemy in your house!

referring to the foreign guest as the enemy. With this, he was basically calling tourists the enemy and supporting the fact that owners of the rental place should not trust guests and should be reporting anything suspicious to the state. Holistically looking at operational efficiencies, it is interesting to think about how the quality of services at hotels and *casas particulares* could be improved if managers in charge stopped wasting their time searching rooms, tracking guests, and performing background checks.

The current challenges in healthcare, tourism, and agriculture and food production are impacting everyday life decisions made by Cubans. From an outside point of view, one may conclude that the root cause of these challenges is the Cuban Government's mismanagement of the Cuban economy. Another view may promote the idea that the sole reason for these challenges is the embargo imposed by the United States. The next chapter will elaborate on the root causes of the current socio-economic realities in Cuba.

CHAPTER V: *EL BLOQUEO EXTERNO E INTERNO Y SUS IMPACTOS EN LA SOCIEDAD CUBANA* – THE EXTERNAL AND INTERNAL EMBARGOS AND THEIR IMPACT ON CUBAN SOCIETY

It is a well-known fact that the United States placed a financial and commercial embargo on Cuba after the 1959 socialist revolution. From the U.S. perspective, the reason for the sanctions was the nationalization of U.S. assets and companies without compensation by the Cuban government. The U.S. blockade continues to this day, and at the time of writing this book, this blockade is enforced through several laws (or congressional acts).

One of the acts enforcing the blockade is the "Trading with the Enemy Act," which authorized sanctions on Cuba in 1962 for three reasons: the lack of compensation to the U.S. for the nationalization of U.S. properties and assets in Cuba, the Bay of Pigs invasion, and the Cuban Missile crisis.

The other prominent act is the infamous "Cuban Liberty and Democratic Solidarity Act of 1996," which is also known as the Helms-Burton Act because it was introduced by North Carolina Republican senator Jesse Helms and by Republican representative of Indiana, Dan Burton. This act attempted to prohibit any non-American international companies from doing business with Cuba by subjecting them to legal action and banning their leadership from entering the U.S. This entry ban had a large impact on major stockholders of companies that are doing business with Cuba. This particular provision in the act aims to force companies to consider their trade volumes and transactions with the U.S. in comparison to those with Cuba and ultimately to choose between doing business with the U.S. or Cuba (Frank, Tougher U.S. sanctions make Cuba ever more difficult for Western firms, 2019).

Sherritt International is a Toronto-based Canadian mining company that has a joint venture operation with the Cuban government in the Pedro Soto Alba Nickel mine in the region of Moa, located in the eastern province of Holguín. In 1996, the U.S. government banned senior executives and their families from entering the U.S. because of the company's business relationship with Cuba. In 2019, significant problems began to hit Sherritt International. They faced operational challenges due to a shortage of fuel at the Moa mine and began to have issues with accounts and receivable payments due to U.S. sanctions. In fact, Sherritt's nickel mine has a certified claim of $88.3 million (close to its market capitalization in 2020) as the revolutionary government expropriated the Moa mine in 1960 from a U.S. New Orleans company, "The Moa Bay Company" (Wicary, 2019). The claim is possible under the Helms-Burton Act Title 3, which gives the green light to sue any entity that traffics in property confiscated by the Cuban Government.

The embargo, what the Cubans refer to as *el bloqueo*, has restricted U.S. exports to Cuba and, as the Sherritt International example shows, restricts investment. As a result, a company with extensive operations or market presence in the United States will not risk losing billions of dollars of business with the U.S. versus only a few hundred million dollars of trade with Cuba. It is hard to compete with the economic powerhouse that is the United States, with a GDP of nearly $20 trillion in 2020, versus a sanctioned and state-controlled economy with a GDP of $100 billion.

The U.S. embargo has impacted the Cuban economy over the last half-century, with the impact being more pronounced during and after the Special Period. The embargo is a fixed constraint in Cuba's economic equation. However, over the past three decades, there have been insufficient efforts put forward by Cuba to resolve the fundamental problems arising from this embargo.

As discussed, in previous chapters, the necessities of people, such as the availability of food at affordable prices, have not been adequately addressed.

At a time when the Cuban government is faced with a liquidity crisis, $2 billion annually is escaping from Cuba's Central Bank account to purchase food that should have been produced internally. Cuba, with its vast territory and fertile land, has not invested sufficiently in the infrastructure to advance farming, nor has it planned or invested enough to farm chicken, beef, and other livestock. Increased farming efficiency and overproducing livestock, grains, and vegetables at economies of scale would reduce prices and ensure an abundance of food for the Cuban people. Cuba could very well look into its South American partners, such as Uruguay, Paraguay and Brazil, and leverage technologies and know-how. As top cattle producers in the world, these countries could offer valuable support to help Cuba set up its own industry and combat climate-related challenges associated with cattle production. This would be a permanent solution to help reduce the $2 billion currently spent on importing food. Furthermore, because Cuba is surrounded by ocean, it has the ability to not only satisfy demand in Cuba but be a leading exporter of fish. I believe that the limited availability of food is one of the leading root causes of socioeconomic issues in Cuba. When such a large percentage of one's budget is spent on food, this clearly needs to be the first step in attempting to cure the ailing Cuban economy.

It might be helpful to present a famous psychology theory that is well referenced in both business and academia to explain the behavior caused by the scarcity of food in Cuba. Maslow's hierarchy of needs (Maslow, 1943) is a psychology theory by Abraham Maslow that explains how we as humans prioritize some behaviors over others, and identifies the triggers or conditions that cause said behaviors. In essence, our needs determine our behavior. This pyramid of needs (Figure 3) consists of five layers, which outlines that to progress through the hierarchy, one has to first meet the needs at the lower level.

Figure 3. Maslow's Hierarchy of Needs

This hierarchy of behavior explains that one must first fulfill physiological needs before traversing to the next layer... safety needs. Subsequently, one must have safety before moving on to a sense of belonging and love.

The scarcity of food at unaffordable prices in Cuba creates a mentality and a motive for people to first resolve their "physiological needs," according to Maslow's hierarchy. Thus, the main focus for most people would be to satisfy the first layer of Maslow's hierarchy of needs, and as a result, people do not have the time or the energy to focus on higher layers of the hierarchy.

According to research conducted and published in the Journal of Nutrition, loss of overall productivity, psychological suffering, and illness are the implications of food insecurity, lack of adequate food supply, and variety (Anne-Marie Hamelin, 1999). Lack of food variety often leads to malnutrition, because people are consuming fewer vegetables and/or reusing fried oil to save money. Reused fried oil releases acrolein, which is a carcinogenic compound (Overused cooking oil may promote cancer progression, 2019). Malnutrition, of course, has health impacts, which in turn has negative effects in the near term, while increasing the probability of heart attacks, cancer, and other illnesses in the longer term. Malnutrition also causes immense strain in the healthcare system, forcing the government to spend more on treating people. There lies a conundrum. Should the government prioritize its investments to provide an adequate, diverse, and affordable food supply for its citizens and prevent diseases such as cancer? Or spend the money on healthcare for treating patients?

It is paramount that Cuba achieves food self-sufficiency in order to address these underlying problems. It should not be hard. Food self-sufficiency is something that is in line with the characteristics of a socialist state, and it should be made a priority.

Apart from the challenges around food self-sufficiency, the necessary infrastructure is disastrous. Movement within the country is restricted and is very costly, namely because of fuel shortages, limitations in available inter-city transportation, and lack of general infrastructure. As discussed earlier, high transportation costs directly impact the prices of products that the farmers sell in the cities. Recent efforts have been made to revive the railway system in Cuba using help from China. The idea was also put forth to set up a high-speed train from Havana to Varadero with assistance from Russian Railways (Mario Fuentes, 2019). However, there is no concrete and long-term plan to improve the country's transportation infrastructure (Carlos A. Penin and Sergio Alfonso, 2009).

Due to the sanctions, Cuba's national carrier, Cubana de Aviación, does not have enough planes to cover domestic needs, and aircrafts are often delayed, or internal flights are often canceled to give priority to international flights. The main highway in the country (La Carretera Central), which runs from the far west to the far east, is in disastrous condition. The highway is somewhat functional from Havana to the city of Santa Clara, but as you approach Santa Clara, there is no division between same-direction and oncoming traffic, making it impossible to distinguish which side of the highway you are on. After the city of Santa Clara, the government ran out of money and decided to just leave the highway as a two-lane country road, which continues for 600 km (370 miles) to Santiago de Cuba. The highway is not maintained at all, and every so often, the driver needs to zigzag to avoid potholes. Many people have died as a result of accidents on this narrow road, which farmers and other cars are forced to share.

It isn't just the transportation sector that is in dire need of infrastructure upgrades, as almost every sector of the Cuban economy is in need of revamping. Even though the embargo hurts the Cuban economy, the Cubans have also sanctioned themselves by not attempting to overcome some of the main issues that would have potentially eased the pain of the U.S. sanctions. This self-sanction is dubbed the "internal *bloqueo*."

The external and internal *bloqueos* have impacted both Cuban society and socioeconomic values. Going back to Maslow's Hierarchy of Needs, society needs to satisfy the physiological necessities for food, adequate shelter, clothing, and water to be able to traverse to the next layer. The next layer in Maslow's hierarchy is safety and security, which includes security in one's employment that compensates and motivates a person to be able to cover his or her daily expenses. Certainly, the physiological need and safety/security needs are the prerequisite to traverse to the next hierarchy, which is the sense of connection and family. Unfortunately, mainly due to the limitation in satisfaction of the first two essential steps in Maslow's hierarchy, most of the families are broken, and the divorce rate in Cuba is one of the highest in the world (DePaulo, 2019).

Furthermore, the problems associated with the first two essential steps of Maslow's hierarchy cannot be addressed from one generation to the next, because Cubans do not have the means to accumulate wealth during their lifetime. As a result of low average wages and high expenses in Cuba, people simply cannot save money or accumulate wealth through various asset classes and systematically transfer wealth from one generation to next. In other words, the previous generations cannot accumulate wealth because of their low salaries, and the only valuable tangible asset that they can pass on is the family house.

The lack of adequate spending on the agriculture and transportation infrastructures in Cuba forces the people to spend a high percentage of their daily lives struggling to guarantee food for their families and getting from one place to another. These tasks take a lot of time from Cubans and do not give them a chance to focus on creating essential businesses or inventions that could benefit their families and their country. In other words, Cubans have no time or energy left to focus on priorities other than things which should have been solved by the government: the essentials. This situation impacts everyday decisions made by the Cuban people about which profession they should pursue, which aspirations they should have, and what to do to survive. Because of limited opportunities in Cuba, people's choices are often limited as well. As a result, they may not live their full potential or use their talents to contribute to society. Consequently, the External and Internal *Bloqueos* impact not only the country's economic situation but also Cuban society as a whole.

I have met many folks who have to deal frequently with the limitations caused by the *bloqueos*. There are stories of perseverance, hope, despair, success, and failure all across the country. I have come across many eye-opening stories from different parts of Cuba, but there are two that stand out, that have touched me profoundly and give an insight into the effects of these *bloqueos*. I'd like to bring to light the stories of two young women who showed tremendous courage and perseverance. To preserve their privacy, I will call them María and Bárbara.

María is a young woman who lives in the eastern province of Holguín, in one of the smaller municipalities of this province. She comes from a humble background, her mom being a cigar factory worker with a meager salary of $42 dollars monthly, and her dad being a construction worker for the state. Her father, who attempted to branch off and start his own house renovation business, ended up with only one or two contracts. Because María's family lives in a small municipality, there is not much work needed as most do not have the money even to repair minor items in their houses. Even if they had the money, María's father would not have made more than $100 per month, out of which he would have to pay more than 25% to the government because of the license tax. The family relies on the remittance from María's half-sister, Ana, who left the country to help them out financially. At the time of writing this book, María's family can buy their food with the well-needed remittances sent by Maria's half-sister, yet receiving them has become increasingly difficult due to the augmented sanctions on Cuba and the closure of Western Union branches across the country.

However, even with the remittance from abroad, the family cannot eat chicken or meat frequently, and instead, they resort to rice, mayonnaise, beans, and plantains. Though still challenging, the family's financial condition is much better than five years ago when Ana was still living in Cuba. Ana, who now lives in Spain, was brought up in a much different environment than María, as obtaining food during the Special Period was a challenge for a family with no source of income and which sometimes went without food for dinner. As a result, Ana, at the age of 16, moved to Havana to figure out a way to help out her cash-strapped family. Upon her arrival in Havana, 16-year-old Ana found a job that would often pay her twice the salary of a factory worker in a day. It was a job that has existed since the beginning of time, and it is the oldest profession in the world. Havana was the ideal spot for her work, as it is considered the number one destination for foreign tourists in Cuba. The horrific stories associated with her work, which I won't elaborate on here, have had a tremendous psychological impact on Ana. Anxiety, depression, suicidal thoughts, and a lack of interest and motivation were amongst the many traumas affecting her emotional state.

These impacts were ever-present until Ana met an older European man in his 70s who fell in love with her and eventually married her. She finally found a way out of the country and into Europe, where obtaining a visa is almost impossible if you don't have an official job or a property under your name. If you are a younger woman, the probability of obtaining a visa is even slimmer. Ana has since started her own business in Europe while supporting her family of five at home. Ana is the reason why her sister can now go to medical school instead of worrying about the financial difficulties that once impacted her family when Ana was young.

María always had a vision of becoming a doctor and traveling abroad on a medical mission. She wanted to become a doctor, not only for social prestige or the slightly higher salary or the perks that the Cuban government typically provides to doctors, but because she believes in helping people and saving lives. María, who is currently studying medicine in her final year, has gone through very tough challenges as a medical student, including the fact that she walks to her school, which isn't close, under the scorching sun. One instance of María's determination is the time that her pens, which were provided by the government, were all out of ink. In order to do the work required of her, writing in the patients' folders, she bought pens for herself by saving money that should have been spent on food. In my opinion, this was the least of her challenges as a medical student. The biggest problem that I saw is that María had no medical gloves during medical examinations, so she was consistently reusing and resterilizing the gloves used before. At times during her hospital training, she had to conduct examinations without gloves. As a result, Maria's hands were infected with "tinea manuum" or fungal dermatitis infection because of her inability to protect herself during a medical exam.

Believe it or not, it doesn't end there. When María gets home from work, she has to share a room with her *sobrino*.[14] She has to study on her bed at her house that does not have A.C. Her room does not have a door—just a curtain. She has no privacy to study, and it is challenging for her to concentrate on her projects in the field of medicine, which is demanding. To exacerbate things, she cannot afford a laptop to do her assignments, and if she could afford one, there is no official store that sells laptops in her town. As a result, she needs to rely on her sister from abroad. María's

---

[14] Nephew.

mother and father would prioritize their food and would give more portions to María and her nephew so that they would be able to focus on their studies and get ahead. At times, even with Ana's help, María's family may not be able to afford to buy all their necessities. Life definitely could have been more challenging for María and her family, had it not been for Ana supporting them from Europe. Despite these hindrances, she has attained the highest grades in her class and has participated in cultural events and cultural dance competitions organized by her university. Her goal is to become one of the top ophthalmologists in the entire country.

Unfortunately, because of the internal *bloqueo* and lack of economic infrastructure and economic planning in the eastern provinces where María and Ana are from, there are no opportunities for jobs, growth or economic prosperity. Lack of opportunities and malnutrition were the driving force for Ana's move to the more prosperous occidental part of the country, in this case, Havana, to become a sex worker. The lack of economic planning has also led to the unavailability of basic supplies in hospitals. Guaranteeing essential and low-cost items is paramount, as items like pens and medical gloves are the tools that the doctors, interns, and medical staff need to conduct their everyday jobs.

Then we have Bárbara, a single mother who separated from her boyfriend a year after her daughter was born. When she was 17, she fell in love with her then-boyfriend, a taxi driver, and moved out of her house to live with him. In Cuba, during the uptick in tourism in early 2000, anyone who had a vehicle could apply for a taxi license.

Bárbara, who was a talented musician in her pre-university years, left her career as her new boyfriend, who happened to be 15 years older than her, convinced her not to continue her studies because he needed her most at home to take care of house chores. He was quick to mention that her music and singing career was not going to give her any money in the long run in comparison to what he was making. She was shut down and told not to waste her time because she wasn't going to make anything anyways, with her making a monthly salary that her boyfriend would make in two hours.

Unfortunately, being young, naive, and easily influenced by the love of her life, she did not continue her university education, which is free of charge in Cuba. Despite the harsh disagreements from her parents and their criticism of Bárbara leaving her university studies, she still chose to live at her boyfriend's house. Bárbara's relationship started to change only after a year of living with him. Her boyfriend was physically, emotionally, and sexually abusive and this behavior was exacerbated as he consumed alcohol.

Bárbara tried to escape from her boyfriend's house many times and went back to her parents' place, but Bárbara's parents, not knowing the truth, forced her to go back to her boyfriend's house. The abuse occurred daily and was a reality that she considered part of her life. It was as if she was now conditioned to accept this toxic way of life as something normal.

The trend of these abuses continued until Bárbara, who was undergoing severe depression, had a breakthrough, a breakthrough that happened when she became pregnant with her daughter. Bárbara was planning her escape right before she was pregnant, but this time she did not plan to go back to her parents' home. Instead, she chose to escape to another province. The psychological abuse continued throughout her pregnancy. She eventually managed to successfully escape the abuse and returned to her parents' house with her daughter, but one night, her drunk boyfriend showed up with a knife, threatening Bárbara's entire family. It had reached a point that she was scared to leave her house, so she approached the police for help. The police had supposedly put a restraining order against Barbara's ex-boyfriend, which he kept violating daily without any consequence from the police. Even after several instances of approaching the police, their response to her was: "Please find yourself another man who would go and show a lesson to your abusive boyfriend, so he is never able to abuse you again."

Since then, she has courageously overcome many of her fears and depression as a result of years going through therapy. Bárbara has started her own home business, and her daughter has begun to focus on music in middle school. As a hobby, Bárbara is planning to start a band with her former pre-university classmates who are now professional singers to produce their album and market their music at the national level.

These are two stories that have personally touched me, and I commend these brave women. They demonstrated the courage to recover, the courage to get back up again, and the courage to have a breakthrough point and say enough is enough. Bárbara, Ana, and María dared to push through and overcome their challenges without any idea about the direction life was going to take them. They exhibited great strength by moving forward and overcome fears and hardship, even though the laws protecting these brave women were not fully enforced.

The North American legal system has created an environment where women's rights are protected by correct and impartial enforcement of the law. The evolution of our laws and, most importantly, the enforcement of these laws, has limited abuse and defended women's rights, which is something that we can sometimes take for granted.

While Cuba has strict rules and regulations in place, they are not enforced consistently, equally, and in a ubiquitous fashion. In these two examples, the law to protect a woman from her abusive boyfriend existed but was not adequately enforced. The police officer's suggestion to outsource his or her duty by telling Bárbara to find another boyfriend to defend her is simply unacceptable. There are other situations where laws are in place but not thoroughly enforced. For example, in Cuba, given that the age of consent is 16 years old, there have been cases (predominately in the countryside) where older men of more than 50 years old engaged in sexual relations with minors who were 16 years old or even younger.

Law and order are not important just because it is right or socially just. The rule of law and strong institutions are vital to protect property rights, and essential for the success of business and land ownership. A government capable of guaranteeing that laws are fully enforced would minimize the risk of doing business in Cuba, which, in turn, would attract investment. In Cuba, the law of property and business ownership exists, but it is not fully enforced. Cuba has made gradual improvements to create an environment where private businesses can form, allowing the purchase and sale of houses in 2011.

Going forward, as Cuba opens itself up gradually to more investments, property and business ownership rights will be key to attracting and keeping investors. As discussed earlier, Helms-Burton Title 3 allows companies whose properties were confiscated during the revolution to be able to sue any entities using their properties in Cuba. The activation of Helms-Burton Title 3 gives the green light to a certified claimant or U.S. national, or a non-certified claimant of a Cuban national who later on became a U.S. citizen (Act, 1996). The activation of this act has impeded companies wanting to conduct business with Cuba and has put pressure on Cuba to gradually open up its doors for business. However, despite the current challenges that Cuba faces, ensuring that property ownership rights are fully observed and implemented will create a positive environment for future business opportunities and foreign investment.

To summarize, the pressure on Cuba's economy is not only caused by external reasons like the sanctions, *el bloqueo*, or the Helms-Burton Act. These have undoubtedly caused severe negative impacts on the economy and have made life difficult for Cubans. It is clear that the embargo puts Cuba on an uneven playing field when it comes to the international business stage.

As much as the external *bloqueo* causes pain for Cuba, there is certainly an internal *bloqueo* as well. Addressing the internal *bloqueo* is important to create significant change. Analyzing its consequences, which have impacted Cuba's infrastructure, laws, and business opportunities, is the focus of this section. Next, we dive into some plausible solutions that can be implemented in order to once again make Cuba the jewel island of the Caribbean.

CHAPTER VI: RECOMMENDATIONS FOR ECONOMIC RECOVERY

"La crítica es el ejercicio del criterio: destruye los ídolos falsos, pero conserva en todo su fulgor a los dioses verdaderos".

"Critique is the exercise of judgment: it destroys false idols, but preserves the true gods in all their brilliance."

José Martí

There is most definitely a lack of vision for the future that seems to be holding Cuba back. I once had a career mentor that used to ask me what I wanted to be when I grew up. I was surprised by the question because, at the time, I was a Master of Engineering student and was simultaneously working at BlackBerry. Nonetheless, I sought his advice, because I wanted to keep progressing in my career. I wanted a change that would get me ahead, but I lacked the vision to come up with a concrete plan. The purpose of my mentor's question was to put me on the spot to think about my vision for the future and where I should leverage my skills to be competitive and achieve my goals.

Having a vision is the most fundamental step for creating change, as that vision will become the reason why change is necessary. The justification for change, in turn, leads to the development of a plan. Applying the same concept to Cuba, I believe the more fundamental issue is not the sanctions or economic problems, but rather the big picture question of what Cuba wants for its future.

From the government's perspective, Cuba's current vision involves maintaining a socialist economic system and an ability to makes its own independent decisions about its affairs, free from outside influences and dominance. The pressing question is: how well is this vision holding up and is it a sustainable way to create a prosperous future for Cuba?

Is Cuba's current vision for its economy to continue the same pattern of food rationing, where there is no adequate supply of chicken, milk, or other necessary products for its people? Is the vision to provide so-called free healthcare that does not cover basic necessities and encourages people to slip a $5 or $10 bill under the table to skip the long hospital lines and get a better service? Is the vision to spend millions of dollars on free education and not reap the benefits of the enormous talent that Cuba has? Is the vision to spend 12.8% of its GDP annually on education while the educated population cannot find a job in their field, forcing brain drain to occur, yet expecting to improve industries with a reduced number of trained professionals? Is the vision to continue to export items that do not have any competitive advantage in the world market?

Cuba needs to ask itself whether repeating the same band-aid solutions and perpetuating the *status quo* over and over again and expecting different results will lead to a better outcome for its economy.

There are many shortcomings in Cuba's current vision, even though the government has attempted to circumvent the embargo and improvise economic decisions on the fly. For example, infrastructural investments are not diversified in other sectors of the economy, so Cuba relies on foreign family remittances and cellphone recharging, which constitute approximately 5% of its GDP. Furthermore, the GDP per capita is around $8,000 USD, while the average worker takes home $42 per month. There is also no consistent plan to modernize or repair infrastructure. The government will renovate, paint, and clean up the structures in the tourists areas or buildings surrounding the road where Pope Francis' car passes through on a visit, but families living two streets away do not see the money to be able to do a facelift on their house or their neighborhood.

It seems to be about portraying a vision and quality infrastructure rather than actually having it. When the Cuban president visits a school, it is not uncommon to have the school director and other managers make sure that everything looks perfect, seeking not to reveal the truth about the shortcomings to the president, such as kids passing out from malnutrition. The current vision looks like advertising a hotel as five-star and charging five-star prices while rendering one-star service. All in all, it is clear that the current *status quo* has not resulted in a positive turnaround of Cuba's economy, nor does it have a positive impact on the current Cuban socio-cultural status.

Thus far, Cuba's overall economic solutions have not been concrete, except for the decision to open up the country to tourism out of desperate need during the Special Period. The solutions to the economic problems have so far been band-aid type solutions whereby something breaks, and they apply a temporary fix rather than focusing on the fundamental problem. This is why it is all the more important to attempt to achieve self-sufficiency and satisfy the country's essential needs.

During the Soviet era, Cuba was enjoying subsidies and help from the Soviet Union, and the Soviet Union was providing Cuba with oil for its energy needs and oil-dependent machinery for agricultural and industrial purposes. Once a great thing for Cuba, this help from the Soviet Union created an oil-dependent society. The country's energy dependency truly manifested itself during the Special Period after the collapse of the Soviet Union, when the Russian Federation stopped the shipment of oil to Cuba. The shortage of fuel resulted in electricity not being generated at the level that was being demanded, leading to frequent power outages across the country. More importantly, fuel shortages impacted Cuba's food production on farms because there was no gas to operate the farm vehicles. This is like taking the sun away from the planet. In this case, taking away the principal source of energy, oil, caused power outages, food shortages, mass starvation, and the closing of factories. The shortage of gasoline had also paralyzed the transportation system, resulting in an average waiting time of two hours in each direction just to get to work. The Special Period forced Cuba to make some very bold decisions regarding opening up to tourism, offering farmland to farmers for free, and manufacturing organic pesticides. The Special Period forced people to use their rooftops and gardens to grow vegetables and raise livestock, mainly chickens and pigs. People were obligated to be inventive and create their micro eco-farms.

A big moment in history occurred in 1998 towards the end of the Special Period (1991-2000). The economic shock of the Special Period was stabilizing, and Cuba began to improve its relationship with the newly elected socialist president of Venezuela, Hugo Rafael Chávez Frías.

Venezuela had supplied crude oil to Cuba under the "Oil for Doctors" program, through which Cuba sent over 30,000 medical personnel and dentists to work and train Venezuela's medical staff in exchange for oil, which Cuba badly needed to keep its struggling economy afloat. However, after Chávez's passing, the decline in oil prices, from over $100 per barrel in June 2014 to just below $30 per barrel in February 2016, had impacted Venezuela's economy and caused massive hyperinflation. In 2019, because of increased U.S. sanctions on Venezuela, there was a slight reduction in the shipment of oil to Cuba, which had caused long lineups at the pump in Cuban cities, frequent power outages, reductions in factory production, and disruption in transportation because of fuel shortages. The supply was replenished at a later date, even though Venezuela was going through an economic crisis of its own.

This series of events proves that, just like the majority of countries in the world, one of Cuba's biggest problem is an energy problem, where only a small blip in the oil supply can cause long lineups at gas stations and factory shutdowns. Cuba's daily oil consumption is around 172,000 barrels (Independent Statistics and Analysis, 2016), with an internal production of nearly 50,000 barrels per day in the province of Matanzas (Administration, 2015). Because Cuba has to import oil from Venezuela, any disruption in the energy supply can result in economic problems for the country.

This energy dependency has influenced Cuba's foreign policy decisions, specifically with Venezuela and historically with the former Soviet Union. Even though Cuba is aware of this dependency, the decision to become self-sufficient has not been at the forefront of their policy initiatives. There are plans to generate 24% of its electricity needs from renewable sources by 2030 (Vermeer, 2017), which is a step in the right direction, but this is still not enough at this point.

While it's not possible to eliminate energy dependence, it is possible to take steps to reduce this dependency and prepare for more capacity in anticipation of future economic expansion. Independence and striving for a better future have always been the dream of the Cuban people. It is my belief that Cuba should focus on addressing problems that are fundamental to the success and self-sufficiency of the country, which will ultimately create a prosperous future.

Sanctions exist, and yes, times have been tough. Energy is definitely a major issue. But the fundamental question remains: What is Cuba's vision for its future? What type of actor does it want to be in the highly competitive global market? How can it rescue itself from the economic crisis without jeopardizing its values, integrity, and dignity? This is not an attempt to compare socialism versus capitalism or to propose a Vietnam-like recovery model. A new economic model only comes after deciding the fundamentals of who they want to be as a society.

It is my belief that Cuban citizens should have a role in choosing the policies and affairs that will lead to a more prosperous nation, especially when we consider how the country gained its independence. The Cuban people would like to see a continuation of free medical care for everyone, a continuation of free education, and a separation of church and state. Based on my first and second-hand accounts, Cubans would also like to see the continuation of their vibrant music culture and of a society where different races and sexes are treated equally. However, they would like these positive aspects of their economy and social life maintained, only with a significant improvement in the quality of life, management, and policies. With a new vision, Cuba would have a roadmap to get back to the level that Havana once had, when it was an influential actor in global trade in the 19th century. Solidifying a vision, focusing on energy and food supply, investing in infrastructure are all steps in the right direction.

It is important that the vision forward has a clear direction and demands higher quality in regard to the areas of opportunity that already exist in Cuba. For example, the medical programs must be of exceptional quality, where relatives of employees don't have to bring supplies from the U.S. or Canada. As the American football coach Jimmy Johnson puts it, "The difference between ordinary and extraordinary is that little extra." This vision calls for that little extra. With it, I am confident that Cuba can transition from ordinary to extraordinary.

The vision is an independent Cuba that will find itself again on the world stage and contribute to the global economy through new and novel technologies, while increasing quality of life and prosperity in Cuba. One of the first steps to achieving this vision is to determine methods to combat the economic crisis immediately, and fundamentally address these profound challenges. To achieve this goal, first and foremost there needs to be an increase in the country's GDP and a positive Balance of Payments.[15] In other words, Cuba needs to increase its revenues and exports to be able to invest in its human capital, infrastructure, and dominate a strategic niche in the global market.

By focusing on high-quality goods or services that could be produced at low costs, Cuba could achieve economies of scale and capture demand. The highest traded commodity in the world after crude oil is coffee, and Brazil has found a niche to become the top coffee-producing country. Cuba can find a similar niche in international markets and dominate that niche to increase its Balance of Payment. This concept worked for Brazil with coffee and beef, and it can work for Cuba in other fields. (Mano, 2019)

In order to achieve prosperity and resolve its current economic problems, Cuba needs to leverage and focus on its competitive advantages. One of these advantages is that Cuba has low labor cost, which can result in a lower price of manufactured goods in comparison to similar products manufactured in the western world. In a socialist economic system, the elementary factors affecting production (Capital, Instrument of Labour, and Workforce) are controlled by the government. In other words, the government invests the capital and employs the workforce. Workforce compensation is generally lower in comparison to that of the free market economies, as a result of the justification that the government provides its citizens other essential services for free (such as free healthcare, education, and subsidized housing), that the workforce would not need to spend its earned wages on.

---

[15] A country's Balance of Payments refers to the difference between the money flowing into it and the money flowing out to the rest of the world in a particular period of time.

Cheaper labor prices in comparison to those in North America have made socialist China into the world's factory. China's lower labor costs in comparison to those in North America and Europe have made finished manufacturing products cheaper than when manufactured in North America or Europe. Cuba can follow in the same footsteps as China. Because of its lower labor costs in comparison to that of China, Cuba can manufacture certain products at a cheaper cost and can therefore differentiate itself from its potential competitors on the global market.

Given this road map of using Cuba's competitive advantage for manufacturing products at lower prices, Cuba will have the opportunity to dominate the Latin American market and also penetrate to the Canadian and EU markets. Cuba's geographical location and proximity to both the U.S. and Latin America can make Cuba the manufacturing hub of the Americas.

In order to successfully recover from the current economic crisis, Cuba should follow the road map of first addressing the Food, Healthcare and Energy challenges by using future profits from the Manufacturing exports. Furthermore, Cuba would be able to use manufacturing to produce lower-cost domestic necessities such as gloves, syringes, or agricultural machinery, instead of paying hard currency to import these items at higher prices.

The next step on the road map for Cuba's economic recovery is to focus on automation and technology to guarantee competitiveness down the line. In other words, once the investment in the manufacturing sector starts to pay dividends, a move towards high technology is a must in order to stay competitive in the future, and the road to this begins with investing in the Information Technology (IT) sector.

This roadmap outlines Cuba's vast economic potential based on the current status quo, assuming that Cuba would still insist on continuing its socialist economy. The end goal of this roadmap is to bring prosperity to the country by increasing GDP, economic freedom and quality of life for all Cubans.

It is important to note that Cuba's future manufacturing sector would only thrive in conjunction with the solution to other economic problems, like the supply of energy and food and infrastructural expenditure. There is not one component alone that makes an economy thrive, but it is important that we circle back to food, as I believe that this is one of the major players in getting the Cuban economy going. The main issue impacting the number of livestock is the availability of forages, grass, hay, or alfalfa, which are the primary food for livestock. Food availability depends on the Cuban agro-industry, which is very inefficient, both in terms of infrastructure and incentives for farmers. For example, the lack of availability of modern machinery to farm the land has caused hectares of agricultural land in Cuba to grow nothing but weeds.

The solution to address this chain of events is a combination of infrastructure spending, proper management, and incentives for the farmers to gain a profit on a competitive basis. There are certainly challenges to ensuring the availability of high-quality beef and milk, given Cuba's tropical climate. As a result, a serious revamp of agricultural infrastructure and machinery needs to be made to extract the full potential of the arable lands. The new investments in agricultural sectors should first ensure that the food for cattle and livestock is secured. Next, it should ensure that the primary ingredients for Cuban national cuisine are guaranteed. This includes cultivating the foods/ingredients for foods like *plátano maduro frito* (sweet fried plantain), *ropa vieja* (pulled stew beef), *congrí* (rice with beans), *frijoles* (beans), *tamales*, *yuca*, *ajiaco* (soup). The agricultural and agri-food industry should not only ensure the production of the food that meets the minimum demand but instead must aim to produce food at a surplus. Additionally, there has to be adequate planning to cultivate organic vegetables that contribute to a healthy Cuban diet, such as lettuce, celery, cucumbers, and tomatoes. There should also be an emphasis on making currently produced items better. This includes citrus fruits, corn, rice, yuca, soursop, coffee, and tobacco.

Establishing itself as the organic production hub of the world would be a fruitful avenue, because of differentiation against competitors. As discussed earlier, following the Special Period, Cuba had no access to any pesticides and resorted to manufacturing organic substitutes as opposed to conventional synthetic options. There is huge potential and international demand for organic agriculture. By producing in mass quantities, Cuba could not only feed its people but also export, resulting in increased revenues for the country. Achieving economies of scale, lowering labor costs and proximity to the American continent would translate to lower production costs overall. Aside from the cost, the food would be made available at a higher quality and fresh to the consumer, as the short distance between Cuba and the Americas will prevent organic products from perishing. As a result, investment in the agricultural sector and branding this sector as an organic farming center of the world would create a win-win situation for all. This win-win situation would benefit Cuba's economy and health care system, as Cubans would consume more organic, green vegetables, and malnutrition might be reduced because of the availability and variety of food.

Energy is another challenge. Energy is not only a Cuban problem but a worldwide one, as the majority of countries are dependent on imported oil. However, to reduce dependence on oil and fossil fuels, many countries, including some of the top oil producers in the world, have attempted to diversify their energy sources and look for alternative and cleaner energy production systems. The alternatives to fossil-based energy production are mainly nuclear, solar, wind, and geothermal energy sources. As Cuba is an energy-rich country, because of the average of 175 sunshine hours per month, it is ripe for converting the solar energy into electricity using solar farms. Given that Cuba is an island surrounded by sea, it also has the potential to extract wind energy and convert wind energy into electricity. There is already an existing solar and wind infrastructure, providing the potential to save 52,199 tons of fossil fuels. However, there is also a great opportunity to increase this capacity even further, reducing dependence on imported oil and preparing for the future demand that will result from economic expansion and a possible manufacturing boom.

Cuba has an advantage in that the government would be providing the land for solar projects for free. Therefore, spending money on resources, management, updating the old electrical grid system, and massive spending in solar farms and renewable energy is a must to ensure Cuba's long energy problems and power cuts are resolved.

The other challenge that needs to be addressed is healthcare. The primary objective of addressing healthcare challenges is to increase the quality and reach of healthcare. The improved quality would ensure that the "free healthcare for all" mantra is offered at a high quality and is equitable among all patients. All medical equipment must function, be modern, and be readily available, not only in major cities such as Havana, Santiago, and Camaguey but also in rural areas. It is paramount that items like gloves, masks, and sanitization products are accessible to medical professionals. In Cuba, tourists, the rich, the poor, and high-ranking officials should be treated the same and should have the same access to pharmaceutical products. The double standard of better care for tourists at a cost to the Cuban people should be eliminated. Research in the medical and pharmaceutical fields must be funded and expanded and, as the future IT boom (which will be elaborated on next) would revamp the technology infrastructure, telemedicine should provide service to the inhabitants of rural places that may not have the means to travel to the Polyclinics or Hospitals. Finally, the average salary, perks, and incentives of the medical staff should be increased in order to incentivize high-quality work, which would have positive effects in and of itself, eliminating corruption and the clandestine network of selling medicine in underground black markets. The Canadian healthcare system can undoubtedly be used as a successful model, as it spends an average of $7,068 per person annually which adds up to 11.6% of its GDP (CIHI, 2019) while Cuba spends $2,475 per capita on its healthcare system, which represents 11.1% of its GDP (WHO, 2016). As discussed earlier, working under the assumption that the manufacturing sector will receive investment and exhibit growth, the revenue from this sector could easily finance the medical infrastructure in Cuba. Furthermore, with a future focus on telemedicine Cuban doctors can offer their expertise to other parts of the world virtually, not only to add value globally, but also to help the Cuban economy while being able to remain close to their families.

These ideas can supplement the current positive characteristics of the Cuban healthcare system, ensuring that Cuba's international reputation in healthcare is maintained.

Information Technology is also an industry that, I believe, could offer promising opportunities for Cuba, because it involves a lower initial investment in comparison to other sectors and there is a pool of educated talent ready to realize their career dreams. A $2 trillion industry worldwide, one can look at India for a blueprint, as their GDP grew by more than 7%, generating more than $147 billion in annual revenue when they started establishing themselves as a major player in IT (NASSCOM, 2012). The IT industry has had positive impacts on the socio-economic fabric of India as it has created employment in this field. Employment in the IT sector has grown from 284,000 in the year 2000 to 1.63 million in 2007 (Shalini Jain, 2009). IT has helped India to improve its Balance of Payment, with the current account deficit contracting from 4.8% in 2013 to 1.1% of its GDP in 2016 (Banerjee, 2017). Furthermore, more than 10 Indian IT companies are listed on the NASDAQ stock exchange, raising equity capital from investors worldwide.

Because of its time zone and the ability to provide relatively cheap labor, Cuba is well-positioned to respond to demand for labor from the U.S. Information Technology industry. India is well-known as being a place to outsource labor, especially in the IT industry. However, companies often complain about the management, communication overhead and time zone differences, which can cause headaches when performing critical software test and release cycles. Other complaints from U.S. and Canadian companies are the cultural differences that cause communication barriers, as well as physical proximity, which makes it challenging to have in-person meetings.

The human capital in this field is not only talented but also highly motivated. Cuban software talent is desperate for the opportunity to participate in cutting edge technologies and be a part of the global IT trend. It is my belief that the IT industry represents a tremendous opportunity for competitive advantage and a win-win for Cubans and North American companies. For Cuba, the technology sector would employ lots of people, increase social morale, and set an example for the people that tourism is not the only cash cow. The IT sector would end up creating other jobs, such as the construction of new buildings or laying fiber optic cables. Of course, it would also have a net benefit for the U.S. and Canadian banks, high tech, and IT companies. North American companies could save billions of dollars by outsourcing to Cuba, increasing their bottom line. Moving towards IT is promising, as there is potential to increase Cuba's GDP by a minimum of 100%. Instead of taking the tourism approach of charging the companies infinitely more for an employee than what the employee gets paid, the government has an opportunity to collect tax from the companies and employees to guarantee revenues. The government should elect a specific place that needs an economic expansion in Cuba, instead of areas that have already attracted investments. My recommendation, in this case, would be to turn one or all of the following cities into the IT hub of Cuba in priority order: City of Holguín, Baracoa (in the province of Guantanamo), or Bayamo (in the province of Granma). Constant investment in the Occidental part of the country (such as in the Mariel Special Development Zone, Havana, and Matanzas) and neglecting the eastern part of the country is not a great strategy to distribute the wealth and diversify the critical industries on a national level.

Because the government does not have competitive expertise to run an IT business, they should not be the ones partnering up with foreign IT companies. Instead, the government should be encouraging private Cuban enterprises to partner up with the foreign IT entities. According to an article from the Miami Herald (Torres, 2017), this process has already started; it is important that it is explored seriously and systematically. In fact, in December 2016, Cuba and Google took the first step by signing a Memorandum of Understanding (MOU) to improve the internet connection in Cuba. Cuba's connection to the internet is currently through fiber optic cable to Venezuela, causing delays in the exchange of information, but Google and Cuba began the negotiation of the Peering Agreement to connect Cuba directly to Google servers in South Florida and Mexico (Marsh, Google, Cuba agree to work toward improving island's connectivity, 2019). This agreement is the first vital step in ensuring that Cuba is directly connected to Google servers. It is important that, as Cuba interconnects with the infrastructure of the Western world, they simultaneously create an investment-friendly climate where U.S. and Canadian IT companies will want to invest because of low tax rates, free movement of funds, and repatriation of their monies.

With strategic guidance, Cuba can position itself by incentivizing workers to learn certain skills, skills that are poised for growth in the coming decades like Artificial Intelligence (AI) and blockchain technology. Artificial Intelligence will be the highest demand area of information technology that will revamp every aspect of our lives. The idea behind AI is a revolution in computer science to enable computer systems to solve problems by mimicking human intelligence. In other words, AI implements a system similar to the way the human brain works by imitating a system of intertwined and hierarchical neural networks. The AI neural network system would use a large amount of data to learn and optimize a task. For example, an AI system can be given various pictures of a human and the AI computer brain can learn and distinguish between human face picture and a picture of an animal. Once the algorithm has been trained to identify human face patterns, it can then use its learnings to create a new image of a human being that does not exist in reality. AI would minimize the decision-making time and would revolutionize the future by finding patterns, recommending options so that humans can make smarter and faster decisions.

For Cuba to become the IT and AI hub of Latin America, it must meet specific minimum criteria. First and foremost, the government has to acknowledge the need for infrastructure, including connectivity infrastructure, and energy infrastructure. It is also paramount that the Cuban government promotes its AI sector as business-friendly and a low-cost alternative to India and China. The government initially needs to facilitate and encourage technology giants to set up offices in Cuba to hire local talents. Cuba would use this opening to understand future opportunities and trends in the international IT market. Government-subsidized business incubators are a potential bright spot that could not only attract talent but also create sustainable businesses for investors.

An IT hub in Latin America, commonly known as the Chilecon Valley, can lend a hand to Cuba in its search for establishing itself in the IT sector (Thompson, 2015). In 2010, the Chilean government launched "Start-Up Chile," providing equity-free seed capital of up to 50 million Chilean pesos ($65,000 USD) for select companies with functional products, and a year-long visa to start-up a tech business in Chile (Chile, 2020). Currently, Chile ranks first in Latin America for innovation according to the Global Innovation Index ((GII), 2019). Cuba can learn from Chile's experiences in this area to set itself up for success. I suggest that Cuba implements the Chilecon Valley model and provides incentives to the developers but, more importantly, complements these incentives by providing free office space and mentorship. Another opportunity is for Cuba to create an entrepreneurship platform that the entrepreneurs can participate, conduct research, and publish their research papers on, which will advance the flow of knowledge in regard to artificial intelligence and IT. By implementing the aforementioned strategies, Cuba could initiate its climb to becoming one of the main entrepreneurship hubs in the world, not because it mimics the examples of India and China, but because it will offer an environment where start-up companies can fail fast without substantial financial consequences, and succeed subsequently.

The beauty of being a country that has a competitive advantage in AI is that it could add value not only by bringing hard currency into Cuba's economy, but by stimulating productivity and economic growth. This includes areas of opportunity like agriculture, agritech, and energy efficiency. The evolution of Information Technology in Cuba could increase employment, increase the Balance of Payment, and even help rural Cuba with its economic challenges. Rural Cuba can certainly benefit not only in the agritech sector but also in telemedicine, online marketing, and sales and distributions of their products by means of Information Technology.

How would Cuba make its agricultural processes more efficient to increase farm yields? The answer is, quite simply, technology. The use of technology in agriculture ensures that the yield is increased by having data points about the status of the farm. Data points and sensors would need to be placed strategically in the soil to measure soil conditions, moisture level, light, and heat control, and report back to a central system on whether irrigation is required. The automated irrigation system would then come into action and automatically quench the thirst of the crops and prevent them from drying out while minimizing the usage of water. Robotic harvesting would minimize waste and damage to orchards or crops. The beauty of technology and systems like these is that they collect data and build up historical databases. By having massive amounts of data, the simultaneous investment and focus on AI, which was touched on before, would help farmers learn the patterns within the agriculture sector, allowing them to optimize processes. AI can help the farmers identify crop diseases with the click of a button. AI can also be useful in the optimization of the use of fertilizers and identification of which soil and weather conditions would increase the yield of a particular crop. Furthermore, systems like these can be monitored by farmers from their cellphone. It would enable the farmers to focus their attention on making strategic decisions to expand farming rather than being bogged down by inefficient practices.

The initial investment by the Cuban government in agritech may seem significant at first glance. However, the future cumulative value of this initial investment would undoubtedly be higher. As Cuba plans to become the startup hub of the world, there would be no shortage of agritech start-ups, which would help Cuba improve and modernize agriculture at a lower cost. By adapting and modernizing the Cuban agricultural sector, Cuba would expand its livestock production to exceed the demand of internal consumption. Furthermore, Cuba could further optimize crop yields to produce organic fruits and vegetables not only for internal consumption but rather for export to international markets. The emphasis on exporting is recommended only for fruits and vegetables rather than livestock. With the initial investments in the agriculture sector, Cuba would eventually be able to reduce the annual expenditure of $2 billion on food imports.

Similar to agriculture, the energy sector can benefit immensely from AI, leveraging it to optimize energy needs, infrastructure repair, and distribution. AI can help with the predictive maintenance of solar farms and wind turbine systems to minimize the downtime in providing uninterrupted energy to Cubans and future businesses.

Now, all this infrastructural investment and revamping of different industries is not possible without proper management, efficient organizational structure, and efficiency in funding allocation. The organizational, management, and financial structure are the basis for maintaining the quality of any investments going forward. Furthermore, the investments combined with education, training, communicating the new vision to the people, and having everyone on board with the vision are essential for a successful revival of the Cuban economy. I believe we can now add to our vision statement two other essential parts which are: Cuba, the Technology hub, and the organic production house of the world, with accurate planning and efficient management.

I have added the word "efficiency" to the vision statement as it is an essential component to achieving the vision for economic prosperity in Cuba. Let's use an everyday example from our daily lives.

If all of us can do our work more efficiently so that we can save one hour every day, then we would be able to leave an hour early from work (assuming this is possible). We can use that one hour to get a head-start to beat the traffic and return home sooner, or even use that one hour to work out and improve our health or to meditate. Whatever the case may be, saving this one hour by efficiently working would result in 250 hours in one year (calculated as such: 50 work week and five working days per week). If an organization can efficiently save an hour per person every day, it would save 250 hours per year. Assuming an average employment rate of $50 per hour, then the organization will save $12,500 annually per person. Applying the same example to Cuba, if all the industrial processes, farming machines, and light bulbs were energy-efficient, the Cuban government could optimize energy production with less oil consumption. The "little by little" savings would result in more salary in Cuban pockets, and more investments in the healthcare and education systems. Efficiency at all levels is of utmost importance in achieving Cuba's future economic prosperity.

In summary, here is the vision for a new economic roadmap for Cuba which would increase its GDP, ensure a higher quality of life, and promote future economic growth and freedom for Cubans:

1. **Factory of the Western Hemisphere:** Shift to becoming the manufacturing hub of the Western Hemisphere by producing goods at cheaper prices because of the lower labor cost.

2. **Upgrading Ailing infrastructure:** Using the profits from the manufacturing sectors to upgrade ailing infrastructure such as energy, roads, bridges, agriculture and healthcare.

3. **Efficiency and Quality:** As a result of spending on infrastructure and providing incentives to the workforce, Cubans would receive a higher quality of healthcare, food, education.

4. **A shift towards Organic Agriculture and Renewable Energy:** Investment in infrastructure to ensure organic production of food at a lower cost and export to the American

continent. Also, lowering dependence on foreign energy imports and producing electricity from renewable sources.

5. **Technology and AI:** Heavy investment in IT and AI infrastructure to offer services to the rest of the Americas at lowest cost in the global market. The shift to Technology and AI will significantly increase Cuba's GDP.

The consequences of the internal and external *bloqueos* not only caused hardship on the economy but, most importantly, impacted Cuban culture and social dynamics. The economic problems can go away with systematic planning. However, the impacts on the Cuban culture and sociocultural structure would undoubtedly require significant efforts to turn around. The higher divorce rates in Cuba in comparison to other countries are, to a degree, correlated with the *bloqueos*. This, in turn, has impacted the nuclear family structure, which is the fundamental building block of a society. Most marriages, whether registered or through common law, lead to divorce because young couples cannot move out of their house and live independently. Newlyweds often have to live with their in-laws and may have to share the room with other members of the family. High divorce rates in Cuba are caused by infidelity, changing traditional roles in marriage, kids from previous marriages, and lack of understanding of the purpose of the marriage. Growing up in a household where parents are divorced increases the chances of divorce in the marriage as well (Sarah W. Whitton, 2018).

The economic challenges in Cuba have created a false sense of what reality looks like in the rest of the world. Some people think that it is easier to make money in Canada or the U.S. Although this could be argued as true, they do not consider that many folks are unemployed in the U.S., struggling to keep their jobs, and the expenses and financial debt are generally much higher in North America than in

Cuba. Some believe that their family members who live abroad will easily afford to send money to Cuba or buy cellphone packages for them every month. This false expectation is combined with their lack of desire to work in the Cuban job market but enjoy the remittances sent to them from abroad. Certain Cubans may have an inaccurate understanding of what it means and the effort that it takes for the average person to make money in the U.S. This false sense of expectation has created a narrow vision to think and act locally because of the differing expectations. The economic problems in Cuba have conditioned even the very best to not be in touch with the economic reality on a global scale. As a result, their vision has been limited to resolving their day to day life necessities and not having a chance to think globally while acting locally. In other words, the internal and external *bloqueos* have restricted the interactions of the Cuban people from global economic opportunities, a connection that is important to get Cubans to propose plans and solutions to address the demands of tomorrow and an opportunity to dream beyond their own neighborhoods.

The vision that I have proposed is quintessential to revamping the economy towards prosperity. However, there is an important point that needs to accompany this vision to ensure that the government's infrastructural investments would lead to economic success and growth. Without this point supplementing the vision, the government can spend all it desires on the new infrastructure but may not reap the full benefits of the prosperity for people. This critical point is Sociocultural education.

By Sociocultural education, I am referring to essential things that need to be improved, such as law enforcement without corruption, respect for women's rights, an emphasis on family values, and the eradication of "machismo" and violence against women. The most important part of this education is to prevent further disappearance and diminishing of social ethics and values and, most importantly, prevent the spread of harmful values as ethical values. Theft, lies, corruption, and lack of ethics are accepted by some and given legitimacy as the right to struggle and survival and rebellion against the government. It is important that the ideas proposed for transforming Cuban's social norms allow for things like stealing and economic inequality to be addressed.

I understand this thought process may, to some degree, correlate with the economic problems. Still, diminishing ethical values in a society is no excuse, and hence social education is a must. For example, education would promote spending that prioritizes household expenditures and covering a family's basic needs, such as food and wellbeing, before spending money on alcohol. This is the type of education that teaches you not to starve yourself so that you can purchase lottery tickets instead of eating a meal. You may wonder if lottery tickets and gambling exists in Cuba. The answer is yes, but it is all underground, operated in certain houses, and it is distributed across the country.

With the above statements I am not claiming that everyone in Cuba needs to be further educated on these issues, but, based on my observations, there are undoubtedly many socio-cultural challenges that could be addressed. By education, I mean the philosophy of life, values, and responsibility of each person towards society, including norms, traditions, and ethics. I also mean an education that reminds the young Cubans about the reasons for past struggles and shows an optimistic vision for the future. Educating people on the new cultural and ethical identity is important for continuity and is essential to succeed in filling in the gaps and speeding up the process towards a new economic vision. As José Martí once said: "*Ser bueno es el único modo de ser dichoso y ser culto es el único modo de ser libre*"[16]

---

[16] Being good is the only way to be happy, and being educated is the only way to be free.

Restoring prosperity as discussed in this book is not possible without the lifting of the external *bloqueo*. As mentioned earlier, the external *bloqueo* has significantly injured the Cuban economy and prevented the country from fully integrating with the rest of the world. While external sanctions have created a more self-sufficient Cuba in the pharmaceutical sectors, the embargo has only exacerbated the existing inefficient and tumultuous Cuba-U.S. relationship. The removal of sanctions will integrate Cuba back into the world financial markets whereby increased trade, specifically in the IT sector, will be possible. North America will benefit from future organic food production in Cuba at a lower price point because of the reduced cost of production and transport. Vice versa, as hard currency flows to the country, Cubans would slowly gain the trust of international partners and change some of the existing inefficient policies. All that is required is the willingness on both sides to create a win-win situation, as the collective benefit of united cooperation would undoubtedly be more beneficial than their individual gains.

If the entire external *bloqueo* (which again, is the embargo) is lifted tomorrow, would all of Cuba's problems disappear? The answer to this question depends on deeply addressing the internal *bloqueo* head-on. The embargo against Cuba has had devastating impacts, but it is not the only factor impeding Cuba from shining on the world stage.

Over the past few years, I have had the privilege to be able to travel to Cuba, learn about the culture, immerse myself, and experience everything up close. This journey has been a personal learning experience, reminding me to keep an open mind free of bias. Through many years of travel to the island, I have observed a lot of great things and have memories that have touched my heart and taught me invaluable lessons. I have seen a 12-year-old boy in Varadero who brought his eagle every day to the beach, charging the tourists $2 to take a picture of it. Observing him negotiating, running after tourists, or sometimes refusing the tourists' offer because they wanted to get a discount from him made me admire this kid and self-reflect on my fears as well. I chose to become one of the kid's clients, taking a picture with the eagle and chatting with him, getting to know a bit about his story. The kid never gave up on making another buck or two. He had no fear of rejection. He did not read into it too much. He just wanted to make money. The day that I saw him, he probably brought in around $80 cash, twice the average monthly salary of a Cuban worker. The kid taught me a lesson in overcoming fears and persevering. He taught me that the "no's" you hear in life don't really matter. All you need to do is be focused on your objectives.

In the farms near Buenaventura, in the eastern province of Holguín, I had the privilege to know a farmer's family who worked hard to provide a bright future for their daughter Laura. The only child in the family, Laura was 3 years old when she was diagnosed with stage-4 neuroblastoma cancer. This cancer spread rapidly throughout Laurita's entire body and organs.[17] The doctors had told her parents that there was no hope. They had to make many trips to the city of Holguín from their small town, where they did not have the medical infrastructure to support and address Laura's health problems. Despite working hard on the fields planting beans, yuca, mangoes, and raising pigs, sheep, and cows, Laura's parents were not making enough to afford these frequent trips to Holguín. Fortunately, they had family there.

During Laura's ordeal and her battle with cancer, the farm did not provide high yields, and as a result, there was not much to sell to the government, let alone for the family to eat. Laura's parents just wanted to make sure that Laura ate better, hoping it might help her in her battle. Her parents never gave up hope. Her mom says that in a desperate

---

[17] *Laurita* literally translates to 'Little Laura'.

moment, she prayed to the *Virgen de La Caridad del Cobre*[18] and requested her to heal Laura. After a few months, Laura's situation started to improve, and despite the disbelief of both the medical team and her family, she made a full recovery. To this day, in Laura's hometown, they consider her healing to be a miracle. Laura is now sixteen years old and is finishing school, sharing her incredible story whenever she gets the chance. I was impressed by the perseverance of her parents, who never, under difficult conditions, lost their hope.

Stories of love, compassion, perseverance, sacrifice, struggle, and hope can be found all over Cuba. The Cuban people always have their doors open for neighbors, giving them the opportunity to stop in and say hello, enjoy a cup of Cuban coffee, and share their stories from the day. Hugs and kisses are generously exchanged between the neighbors and families. There is always laughter in those conversations, even though times are tough, economically speaking. There is always music in the air, singing, and dancing, and even though there is limited food, neighbors and families get together and are happy with what little they have. The neighbors are like a family who help each other out. The solidarity and unity between the Cuban people are quite incredible, the true definition of humans as social beings. With constant interaction among people, one can rarely get bored or be depressed. They always find ways to make themselves happy and stay positive. Do they wish they had more? Of course. But the point is that their happiness comes from within. Their happiness comes from valuing things in life differently than what we typically value in North America. Cubans, in general, do not necessarily give value to money and tangible items, but rather to friendship, neighbors, children, family reunions, helping a neighbor in need, or a simple laugh. They are persevering and hoping for a better future, and they have a strong desire to alleviate

---

[18] Our Lady of Charity.

the many challenges they face. A positive mentality to make tomorrow better than today, and an everyday feeling of gratitude for the little they have, is what gives them happiness.

For the majority of the Cuban people, there are no worries about paying the car bills, or the mortgage, or college tuition for the kids or insurance policies for loss of life, and loss of work, etc., because they can't access these things to begin with. In Cuba, there are no major debts or credit cards, and their main expenses are food, electricity, and phones. There are no means for people to overstretch themselves by accepting more debt, for example, by financing or leasing a car and then having to work twice as much to pay for a vehicle that they only use 30% of the time. As opposed to people in North America who usually dedicate their efforts to finance depreciable assets, Cubans prioritize their friends and family instead.

Cubans have learned to be content with what they have. Certainly not by choice, they live within or below their means. This way of life makes them more relaxed, less pressured by deadlines. There are many things that we can learn from Cuba. We can certainly learn to be happier with what we have and live within our means. We need to be more caring and supportive, because humans are social creatures that survive and thrive together within a community, and by giving more, we can positively impact others. We can optimize the amount of food we eat so that we do not throw out food in the garbage while kids in Cuba go hungry. We can learn to have a different perspective on life and not to selfishly think that if someone is hungry, it is his or her damn problem.

We can also learn to have a better work-life balance. Do we want to live to work our entire lives, paying bills for unnecessary items that we hardly use? Do we want to immerse ourselves in debt for the useless items that we purchase so that we have to put up with a job or with a boss that we don't like just because we have to pay the bills? Do we want to miss the likes of Valentine's Day dinner or family reunions? Do we prefer being married to our jobs rather than to our significant other?

As I shared my own experiences in Chapter 2, it does not matter how much effort you put as an employee to please your boss so that you can get that next promotion. If you do not spend time with the people you love, you will surely miss them when they are not in your life anymore. There is undoubtedly room to optimize our lifestyle and tune our mentality to value and prioritize family, health, and friendship over work or material things.

We can also learn from the Cubans to be more patient. If we are going through tough times or our salaries are not what we expect them to be, we need to see the positive side of the more important things in life that are valuable but not necessarily tangible, such as health and the people we love. During our toughest times, we need to think about life in Cuba and the smiles on the faces of the people who have a minimum salary, and lack of availability of necessities but optimism for the future.

We need to think about the parents who eat less and even may go to sleep hungry at night so that their kids can eat better to be able to get through school.

At a national level, we can learn not to spend our taxpayers' money on conflicts around the world. We should avoid engaging in conflicts that cost our nations massive amounts of money, money that could otherwise be spent on education, healthcare, and infrastructure at home. Finally, we can learn to apply the idea of making education entirely free for all university students. Free education would prevent the extreme indebtedness of a student who has not even yet begun to make a single dime from his or her university education. Our governments should not view education as an expense but rather as an investment, which ends up leading to innovation and a better economy.

Looking back at Cuba's history, the Cuban people always sought independence and wanted to determine their own future. They are a united and proud people who all dream of leaving a better country for their future generations. The dream of having a better country is evident given the history of Cuba and its struggle for independence, which continues to this day. The Cuban people demand respect and do not tolerate pressure or injustice. Despite the many challenges that they are facing, Cubans are a peaceful people who do not bother anyone or any country. With the future move towards an IT and technology based economy, opportunities are created for young Cubans to dream and one day realize their dreams because of the changes in the country's vision.

My suggestion to you is, if you visit Cuba and if you choose to stay in a resort, please dedicate time to going out and interacting with the people to see how they live. Go in with an open mind, considering that the country is going through challenging times. Form everlasting friendships, learn from their experiences, enjoy the delicious food and the music, immerse yourself in the culture, and finally, reflect on your own experiences. With this work, I hope to have given you a better idea and a glimpse of reality, at least from my perspective, in describing Cuba. Consider my anecdotes, memories, and ideas to account only for 20%. The remaining 80% of your experience will be gained during your next trip to Cuba. Please take my experience above as only one source of truth and perspective. "All models are wrong, but some are useful" (Box, 1976). It is never too late for a paradigm shift. With these considerations, let us all work together to make a better, more just, and more peaceful world to pass on to future generations.

APPENDIX I: SANTERÍA AND THE AFRICAN RELIGIONS IN CUBA

To better understand Cuban society, we need to understand its foundations, including the system of beliefs that people hold. Cuba's most prominent religion is Roman Catholicism, followed by other Christian sects such as Jehovah's Witnesses and Protestantism. Others are of the Santería tradition, which has many followers on the island. Rounding it out, Judaism and Islam have very few followers, constituting about 0.1% of the population (Embassy, 2019).

Going back to the history of slavery in Cuba noted in Chapter 3, the African slaves who were brought to Cuba carried with them their customs and religious practices. African slaves were brought from specific regions in Africa, including Benin, Togo, and parts of Nigeria, and were referred to as the Yoruba people.

The Yoruba people were sold into slavery and brought to the Latin world, to countries such as Cuba, Puerto Rico, Brazil, and Haiti. Slaves worked under harsh conditions in the sugar cane fields, and there was inhumane treatment, including many forms of violence, sexual exploitation, and physical punishments. Whippings were common, and long work hours (often 20 hours per day) and forced sex amongst healthy slave men and women with the purpose of increasing their population were certainly among the most horrific instances of human rights abuses (Miguel Barnet, 1994).

During these harsh times, African slaves faced immense difficulties practicing their religion, as the Yoruba religious belief was criminalized. Slaves could not assemble to practice their religion freely. The Spaniards ultimately perceived the Yoruba religious activities, which involved dancing, animal sacrifice, drums, and music, as evil. As a result, practicing religion was not permitted by the plantation owners. Instead, the slaves were baptized and were forced to convert to the faith of their masters.

The slaves, attempting to adapt to their new realities, congregated and conducted their own religious activities, having them coincide with Catholic holidays or a Saint's birthday. This way, they were conformant with what their masters were celebrating and avoided raising suspicion. As the slaves were forced to convert to Catholicism, they kept their religion and identified similarities syncretized between their new faith (Catholicism) and their ancestral religion (Yoruba). These similarities were often identified between the Yoruba Orishas (or Deities) and the Catholic Saints. For example, in the Yoruba religion, Changó (or Shango), who is the Lord of Fire, Thunder, and War, is syncretized with Santa Bárbara, a brave woman staying loyal and faithful to her Christian belief while being tortured and eventually martyred by her father's sword. Those who believed in Shango and Santa Bárbara celebrated the day of Santa Bárbara's martyrdom on December 4th to avoid raising suspicion. Cubans, who believe in the Yoruba faith, often have statues of Santa Bárbara and Shango on their altars, and offer gifts to these deities such as honey or flowers.

The Yoruba rituals in Cuba often takes place in priests or priestess house. There is a lengthy process to become a *santero* (priest) or *santera* (priestess), starting with spiritual cleansing, receiving a necklace, and going through consultation with *santeros*, before being rebirthed into the

Yoruba faith. The priests and priestesses also need to prove themselves for a year, adhering to a strict set of rules, one of which is dressing in only white clothing for a year, including their underwear and shoes.

If you have ever been to Cuba and have seen someone dressed in all white with beaded jewelry, they are on their journey to become *santeros* or *santeras*. Not all of them follow the rule of dressing in white clothing, however; you will also see yellow and green beaded necklaces and bracelets. The yellow represents the Virgen de la Caridad de Cobre or Oshun, and the mix of yellow and green represents Orúla, the orisha of wisdom and intelligence.

All in all, it is clear that the presence of African religion and Afro-Cuban people on the island has contributed tremendously to the social fabric of the country. The main impact, in my opinion, aside from the religious aspects, is undoubtedly the music and dance. Cuba's traditional music and dance have deep roots in the Afro-Cuban culture.

ACKNOWLEDGEMENTS

The idea and the decision to write this book were inspired by my father, who suggested I transfer my knowledge and travel experiences to Cuba onto others. As I shared my experiences with my family about my trips to Cuba and described the "Symptoms" of what I saw, they encouraged me to dig deeper, to find the root causes and to understand the compelling economic reasons for the shortcomings of socioeconomic problems in Cuba. Without their support and guidance, this book would not exist today.

The main tool that really helped me to gain a valuable experience and interact with people in Cuba was the Spanish Language which I have learned over the years. The first seed of motivation to learn Spanish came from my first trip to Varadero, where I had the chance to observe my brother speaking to the locals. This encouraged me to learn this beautiful language and to interact with anyone I could on the island. Without my brother's encouragement to learn Spanish, and his invitation to join him on his trip to Cuba, this journey would not have been possible.

My first real trip to Cuba outside the resort boundaries is a unique story. As mentioned in the book, I always travelled to Cuba and stayed at the resorts for about 5 to 7 days, and then returned home without any exposure to the *real* Cuba. My first real trip outside the resorts, where I stayed in Cuban cities, occurred years after my first trip described in the book. The reason it happened was that a friend who was supposed to go with me on a trip to Costa Rica, cancelled for personal reasons. I decided to change the destination and fly to Holguín on my first solo vacation. Upon arrival, I made new friends. While I will spare their names for privacy purposes, I will say that they remain close friends to this day, and that they genuinely changed my perspective and assumptions about Cuba, showing me a balanced but fair view of life in real Cuba. Without my friends in Holguín, this experience would have been impossible.

Finally, I want to acknowledge the friends that I have made in Cuba, from Cayo Jutías to Mayarí Abajo, and from Mayarí Arriba to Santiago. For their kindness to share the realities of their daily struggles, hopes and dreams with me, I am forever grateful.

REFERENCES

(GII), G. I. (2019). *Chile ranks 51st among the 129 economies featured in the GII 2019*. New York: INSEAD cornell. Retrieved from GLOBAL INNOVATION INDEX 2019: https://www.wipo.int/edocs/pubdocs/en/wipo_pub_gii_2019/cl.pdf

Act, U. S. (1996). *Cuban Liberty and Democratic Solidarity (Libertad) Act of 1996*. Retrieved from United States - Department of the Treasury: https://www.treasury.gov/resource-center/sanctions/Documents/libertad.pdf

Administration, U. S. (2015). *Cuba Crude Oil Production by Year*. Retrieved from Index Mundi: https://www.indexmundi.com/energy/?country=cu&product=oil&graph=production

Alvarez, O. R. (2019, 03 15). *Cuban Agriculture Still Condemned to a Standstill*. Retrieved from Havana Times (Open-Minded Writing from Cuba): https://havanatimes.org/opinion/cuban-agriculture-still-condemned-to-a-standstill/

Amie M. Gordon, P. (2017, 09 29). *Is Stress Killing Your Relationship? Why You're Not Alone*. Retrieved from Psychology Today:

109

https://www.psychologytoday.com/ca/blog/between-you-and-me/201709/is-stress-killing-your-relationship-why-youre-not-alone

Anne-Marie Hamelin, J.-P. H. (1999). Food Insecurity: Consequences for the Household and Broader Social Implications. *The Journal of Nutrition, Volume 129, Issue 2,*, 525S–528S.

Baker, C. P. (2019, 02 06). *Cuba's Taino People: A flourished culture, believed extinct.* Retrieved from BBC: http://www.bbc.com/travel/story/20190205-cubas-tano-people-a-flourishing-culture-believed-extinct

Banerjee, S. (2017). Analyzing the Balance of payment position of India. *Research Gate*, 36-39.

blogaboutall.ru. (1899). Visitors to the boneyard at Colon Cemetery in Havana Cuba.

Box, G. E. (1976). Science and Statistics. *Journal of the American Statistical Association*, 791-799.

Canada - Cuba Relations. (2018, 05). Retrieved from Government of Canada - Embassy of Canada to Cuba: https://www.canadainternational.gc.ca/cuba/bilateral_relations_bilaterales/index.aspx?lang=eng

Capeci, J. (2004). The Complete Idiot's Guide to the Mafia. In J. Capeci, *The Complete Idiot's Guide to the Mafia* (pp. 138-141). Indianapolis, IN: Alpha - A member of Penguin Group (USA) Inc.

Carlos A. Penin and Sergio Alfonso, J. (2009, 11 30). *Transportation Infrastructure in a Free Cuba: How to Meet Demands in a Challenging Economic Environment.* Retrieved from ASCE - Association for the Study of the Cuban Economy: https://www.ascecuba.org/asce_proceedings/transportation-infrastructure-in-a-free-cuba-how-to-meet-demands-in-a-challenging-economic-environment/

Chile, S.-U. (2020). *Start-Up Chile*. Retrieved from Start-Up Chile: https://www.startupchile.org/

CIHI. (2019). *National Health Expenditure Trends 1975 to 2019*. Ottawa: Canadian Institute for Health Information.

Coombs, R. H. (2004). Workaholism. In *Handbook of ADDICTIVE DISORDERS - A Practical Guide to Diagnosis and Treatment* (p. 368). Hoboken NJ: Wiley and Sons Inc.

Cuba: A New History. (2005). In R. Gott, *Cuba: A New History* (pp. 93-96). New Haven and London: Yale Nota Bene - Yale University Press.

DePaulo, B. (2019, 02 03). *Divorce Rates Around the World: A Love Story*. Retrieved from Psychology Today: https://www.psychologytoday.com/ca/blog/living-single/201902/divorce-rates-around-the-world-love-story

Dubois, L. (March 2004). *Avengers of the New World : The Story of the Haitian Revolution*. Cambridge, Massachusetts: Harvard University Press.

Economics, T. (n.d.). *Cuba - Mean Age At First Marriage, Male*. Retrieved from Trading Economics: https://tradingeconomics.com/cuba/mean-age-at-first-marriage-male-wb-data.html

Embassy, U. (2019, 06 21). *2018 Report on International Religious Freedom: Cuba*. Retrieved from U.S. Embassy in Cuba: https://cu.usembassy.gov/2018-report-on-international-religious-freedom-cuba/

Feinberg, R. (2016). *Open for Business: Building the New Cuban Economy*. Washington D.C: THE BROOKINGS

INSTITUTION.

Foner, P. S. (1963). *History of Cuba and Its Relations with the United States: From the Annexationist to the Second War for Independence 1845-1895*. New York: International Publishers.

Frank, M. (2017, 10 17). *Cuban food output stagnates, may decline in 2017*. Retrieved from Reuters: https://www.reuters.com/article/us-cuba-agriculture/cuban-food-output-stagnates-may-decline-in-2017-idUSKBN1CM1Z5

Frank, M. (2019, 10 09). *Tougher U.S. sanctions make Cuba ever more difficult for Western firms*. Retrieved from Reuters: https://www.reuters.com/article/us-cuba-sanctions-investment-analysis/tougher-u-s-sanctions-make-cuba-ever-more-difficult-for-western-firms-idUSKBN1WO2LP

Gary Clyde Hufbauer, B. K. (2014). Economic Normalization With Cuba: A Roadmap for US Policymakers. In B. K. Gary Clyde Hufbauer, *Economic Normalization With Cuba: A Roadmap for US Policymakers* (pp. 1-11). Washington D.C: Peterson Institute for International Economics.

Gee, K. (2016, 10 12). *America's Dairy Farmers Dump 43 Million Gallons of Excess Milk*. Retrieved from The Wall Street Journal: https://www.wsj.com/articles/americas-dairy-farmers-dump-43-million-gallons-of-excess-milk-1476284353

Gott, R. (2005). *Cuba: A New History* . New Haven, CT: Yale University Press.

Hepatitis may be linked to injections in Cuba. (1991, 06 10). Retrieved from UPI: https://www.upi.com/Archives/1991/06/10/Hepatitis-may-be-linked-to-injections-in-

Cuba/9275676526400/

https://imgur.com/. (1900). American soldiers playing around with human skulls in Colon Cemetery in Havana, Cuba.

Independent Statistics and Analysis. (2016, 07). Retrieved from eia - U.S. Energy Information Administration: https://www.eia.gov/international/overview/country/CUB

JOHNSON, T. (2015, 05 19). *Cuba's dairy industry, once touted as a success, is struggling.* Retrieved from MCCLATCHY: https://www.mcclatchydc.com/news/nation-world/world/article24784696.html

Lawrence, C. A. (2015). Sanctuaries, Border Barriers and Population. In C. A. Lawrence, *America's Modern Wars* (p. 109). Havertown, PA: Casemate Publishers.

Mano, A. (2019, 12 10). *UPDATE 1-Brazil's 2019 beef exports hit record thanks to Chinese demand.* Retrieved from CNBC: https://www.cnbc.com/2019/12/10/reuters-america-update-1-brazils-2019-beef-exports-hit-record-thanks-to-chinese-demand.html

Mario Fuentes, S. M. (2019, 09 13). *Cuba takes first step in railways upgrade with Chinese, Russian help.* Retrieved from Reuters: https://www.reuters.com/article/us-cuba-trains/cuba-takes-first-step-in-railways-upgrade-with-chinese-russian-help-idUSKCN1U900D

Marsh, S. (2019, 08 27). *An island without fish? Cuba aims to tackle problem with law overhaul.* Retrieved from Reuters: https://www.reuters.com/article/us-cuba-fishing/an-island-without-fish-cuba-aims-to-tackle-problem-with-law-overhaul-idUSKCN1VH15Y

Marsh, S. (2019, 03 28). *Google, Cuba agree to work toward improving island's connectivity.* Retrieved from Reuters:

https://www.reuters.com/article/us-cuba-usa-google/google-cuba-agree-to-work-towards-improving-islands-connectivity-idUSKCN1R91ZP

Maslow, A. H. (1943). A theory of human motivation. *Psychological Review*, 370–396.

Mauricio Augusto Font, A. W. (2006). *The Cuban Republic and Jose Marti*. Lanham, MD: Rowman and Littlefield Publishers.

Medina, M. I. (2013, 01 24). *Is Killing a Cow Worse than Murder?* Retrieved from Translating Cuba - English Translators of Cubans writing from the island: https://translatingcuba.com/is-killing-a-cow-worse-than-murder-miguel-iturria-medina-cuba/

Mendoza, J. (2020, 01 07). *Consumption of chicken meat in Cuba from 2010 to 2019*. Retrieved from Statista: https://www.statista.com/statistics/1008780/cuba-chicken-meat-consumption-volume/

Miguel Barnet, E. M. (1994). *Biography of a Runaway Slave, Revised Edition*. Willimantic, CT: Curbstone Press.

NASSCOM. (2012). *The IT-BPO Sector in India*. New Delhi: NASSCOM.

Nguyen, D. H. (2018, 04 30). *Toxic Chemicals in Solar Panels*. Retrieved from Sciencing: https://sciencing.com/toxic-chemicals-solar-panels-18393.html

NUGENT, C. (2018, 11 30). *How Doctors Became Cuba's Biggest Export*. Retrieved from TIME: https://time.com/5467742/cuba-doctors-export-brazil/

Oppmann, P. (2019, 03 27). *Cayo Largo del Sur: Does it have Cuba's best beaches?* Retrieved from CNN Travel: https://www.cnn.com/travel/article/cayo-largo-cuba/index.html

Overused cooking oil may promote cancer progression. (2019, 07 16). Retrieved from IFT Next: https://www.ift.org/iftnext/2019/july/overused-cooking-oil-may-promote-cancer-progression

PADGETT, T. (2019, 06 03). *Cuba Hopes A Catfish Will Solve Its Food Crisis. But Is It Wrecking The Island's Ecosystem?* Retrieved from WLRN: https://www.wlrn.org/post/cuba-hopes-catfish-will-solve-its-food-crisis-it-wrecking-islands-ecosystem#stream/0

Pita GM1, J. S. (2014). Anemia in children under five years old in Eastern Cuba, 2005-2011. *MEDICC Rev*, 16-23.

Press, C. T. (2018, 08 06). *Iberostar raises the bar.* Retrieved from Canadian Travel Press: https://www.travelpress.com/digital_posts/iberostar-raises-the-bar/#.XwacwShKhPZ

Renner, B. (2018, 03 21). *American Families Spend Just 37 Minutes Of Quality Time Together Per Day, Survey Finds.* Retrieved from Study Finds Research, in a nutshell: https://www.studyfinds.org/american-families-spend-37-minutes-quality-time/

Rodriguez Garcia, M., Van Voss, L. H., & Van Nederveen Meerkerk, E. (2017). Selling Sex in the City: A Global History of Prostitution, 1600s-2000s. In M. Rodriguez Garcia, L. H. Van Voss, & E. Van Nederveen Meerkerk, *Selling Sex in the City: A Global History of Prostitution, 1600s-2000s* (pp. 436-439). Boston: Brill.

Rosen, H. R. (2016, 09 19). *"Hep C, where art thou": What are the remaining (fundable) questions in hepatitis C virus research?* Retrieved from AASLD - HEPATOLOGY: https://aasldpubs.onlinelibrary.wiley.com/doi/full/10.

1002/hep.28848

Sarah Marsh, M. F. (2019, 06 04). *Trump administration ban on cruises to Cuba creates chaos for U.S. travelers*. Retrieved from Reuters: https://www.reuters.com/article/us-cuba-usa/trump-administration-ban-on-cruises-to-cuba-creates-chaos-for-u-s-travelers-idUSKCN1T520P

Sarah W. Whitton, G. K. (2018). Effects of Parental Divorce on Marital Commitment and Confidence. *Journal of Family Psychology*, 789-793.

Schneider, E. A. (2018). *The Ocupation of Havana - War, Trade, and Slavery in the Atlantic World*. Williamsburg, Virginia and Chapel Hill, NC: Omohundro Institute of Early American History and Culture and University of North Carolina Press.

Sergio Díaz-Briquets, J. P.-L. (2006). Corruption in Socialist Cuba. In J. P.-L. Sergio Díaz-Briquets, *Corruption in Cuba: Castro and Beyond* (p. 136). Austin, TX: University of Texas Press.

Shalini Jain, D. R. (2009). IMPACT OF IT INDUSTRY ON THE INDIAN ECONOMY. *THE AWARD FOR Ph.D. DEGREE IN COMMERCE & BUSINESS ADMINISTRATION*. MEERUT, India: shodhganga - CHAUDHARY CHARAN SINGH UNIVERSITY.

Strauss, M. J. (2009). Annual Rent Payments. In M. J. Strauss, *The Leasing of Guantanamo Bay* (pp. 126-132). Westport, CT: Praeger Security International.

Stritof, S. (2019, 01 12). *Estimated Median Age of First Marriage by Gender: 1890 to 2018*. Retrieved from The Spruce: https://www.thespruce.com/estimated-median-age-marriage-2303878

Ted A. Henken, M. C. (2013). *Latin America Focus - Cuba*. Santa

Barbara, California: ABC-CLIO, LLC.

Thompson, C. (2015, 05 07). *Three growing start-up cities in South America.* Retrieved from CNBC: https://www.cnbc.com/2015/05/07/three-growing-start-up-cities-in-south-america.html

Torres, N. G. (2017, 03 02). *Cuba has 'largest pool of untapped IT talent in the Americas'.* Retrieved from Miami Herald: https://www.miamiherald.com/news/nation-world/world/americas/cuba/article135249259.html

Vermeer, D. (2017, 08 30). *partnering for cuba's energy transition.* Retrieved from Duke University - Fuqua school of Business: https://centers.fuqua.duke.edu/edge/2017/08/30/partnering-cubas-energy-transition/

Vroom, V. H. (1964). *Work and motivation.* New York: Wiley.

WHO. (2016). *World Health Organization.* Retrieved from UN - WHO: https://www.who.int/countries/cub/en/

Wicary, S. (2019, 04 30). *Sherritt CEO Undaunted by Trump's Tightening of Embargo on Cuba.* Retrieved from Bloomberg: https://www.bloomberg.com/news/articles/2019-04-30/sherritt-ceo-undaunted-by-trump-s-tightening-of-embargo-on-cuba

INDEX

ABOUT THE AUTHOR

Araz Jahani is a Technology Leader in the field of Software Management Consulting with years of experience in AI, Telecom, Energy, and Banking. He holds an Executive MBA from the Rotman School of Management from the University of Toronto, as well as a BA and MA in Computer Engineering from the University of Ottawa and the University of Guelph, respectively, having published multiple conference papers in this field.

Jahani is an avid traveler. During the past ten years, he has visited over 21 countries in order to learn about different cultures, experience different cuisines, and understand the underlying economic issues that shape each destination. He is an advocate for working remotely as a way to explore different cultures while maintaining a steady income.

Since his first trip in 2004, Jahani has visited Cuba numerous times, acquiring an in-depth understanding of Cuban social, cultural, and economic dynamics. His interest goes far beyond economics, however. He enjoys Cuban food, and his list of favorites includes *plátanos maduros fritos*, *congrí,* and *Ropa Vieja*. When in La Habana, he enjoys his afternoon coffee at Plaza San Francisco or Plaza Vieja, and his morning run around the Malecón. When in Holguín, he meets with friends in Parque Calixto García. He can also be found enjoying a refreshing drink on the beaches of Guardalavaca or Cayo Guillermo.

Made in United States
North Haven, CT
08 January 2023

30785035R00076